Purpose in Pain

Purpose in Pain

Rediscovering God's Purpose Through the Pain of Chronic Illness

DAVID HEFLIN

WIPF & STOCK · Eugene, Oregon

PURPOSE IN PAIN
Rediscovering God's Purpose Through the Pain of Chronic Illness

Wipf & Stock
An Imprint of Wipf and Stock Publishers
199 W. 8th Ave., Suite 3
Eugene, OR 97401

www.wipfandstock.com

PAPERBACK ISBN: 979-8-3852-7321-8
HARDCOVER ISBN: 979-8-3852-7322-5
EBOOK ISBN: 979-8-3852-7323-2

VERSION NUMBER 05/04/26

Unless otherwise noted, all emphasis in Scripture quotations is the author's.

To Katie, my beloved wife and partner,
my Paradise in every storm,
my steadfast reminder that all that has been lost
will be made new.

Contents

Preface

TO THE READER WITH CHRONIC ILLNESS

One thing I've learned on my chronic illness journey is that it is always changing. Early in this journey, I would not have been ready to hear anything about purpose in my trials. I am not insensitive to the fact that you, too, are on a journey. However, if you've picked up this book, I assume you are looking for help to hold on to a diminishing supply of hope or a fresh perspective to guide you over the rough and often shifting terrain of chronic illness and pain.

Though this book is ultimately about discovering God's purpose in the midst of our pain, it is structured to acknowledge both our losses and our gains along the chronic illness journey. Honestly, many—and I'm one of them—are too quick to look for divine purpose before they've even accepted what was lost. Short-circuiting the process means you'll have to deal with those losses eventually, and it will be more jarring than if you had dealt with them early on. The part of the book that focuses on losses may be more meaningful for you right now, and at another point of the journey, you might relate more to the part of the book that focuses on gains we experience through chronic illness and pain. The upside is that most anyone who suffers from serious chronic health conditions should find something they can relate to in this book.

The book has two mirroring parts: one emphasizes what we have lost because of chronic illness, and the other emphasizes a corresponding gain on the chronic pain journey. I was inspired by the twin motifs of John Milton's epic poems *Paradise Lost* and *Paradise Regained*.

When God finished his creation masterpiece, he assessed it as "very good" (Gen 1:31). Creation reflected the nature of its Creator. There was nothing impure or diseased in it. The first humans flourished as stewards over the creation to represent God's rule on the earth. The relationships between God and humans, man and woman, and humans and the rest of creation existed in a state of harmony, or to use the common Hebrew word, *shalom*.

The Bible would be a very short book if that were all there was to the story! It didn't take long for Adam and Eve to be seduced by a talking serpent into rebelling against God, who had warned them that such a transgression would result in death (Gen 2:17). We usually think about death only in terms of a body that has expired, but the consequences of death are far reaching.

We see immediately in God's description of the consequences of their rebellion that everything in creation is impacted. If creation's intended rulers rebelled against the Creator, how could the consequences not touch everything? And that's exactly how the Bible portrays the effect. As Andrew Schmutzer describes, "Relational fracture is evident in every part of created life: spiritually, socially, environmentally, and with the personal self."[1]

Therefore, chronic health conditions and all related afflictions are a result of what was lost in the fall of humanity and creation, but even in this chaotic disordering of creation are the seeds of hope. As the apostle Paul says, creation was subjected to futility "in hope that the creation itself will also be set free from the bondage to decay into the glorious freedom of God's children" (Rom 8:21c–22). Setting our personal suffering within the context of the great story of *Paradise Lost* and *Paradise Regained*, we can acknowledge our substantial losses honestly while finding unexpected gains along the way that remind us that all that is lost will one day be regained!

I believe this is a rational way to organize the book, but I do not mean to imply you will always discover an exact gain for what you have lost. Life is never that symmetrical. Reflecting on my own

1. Peterman and Schmutzer, *Between Pain and Grace*, 49.

journey, I have seen truths in both the losses and gains of chronic illness in varying degrees. That doesn't mean they match up all the time, and neither do I expect that they do for you.

Personal Perspectives

I am devoted to following Jesus. I have staked my life on the claim that Jesus is the risen and ascended Lord of all creation, who will raise us from the dead so that his followers can spend eternity with him in a new heaven and a new earth. I expect most of my readers will share these beliefs to a large degree. If you do not share these beliefs or are not fully convinced about them, then it is fair for you to know where I am coming from. I believe that our pain is pointless and unredeemable apart from a good God who makes it count in transformative ways.

I will not say that God caused or even planned your illness or pain. It is within the realm of possibility that he might have, but even if he did, we are rarely privileged to that behind-the-scenes information. Nor will I say that you are better off because you have chronic health conditions. That's between you and God. Those involved with Broken and Mended, our chronic pain and illness support ministry, come from all over the theological spectrum, and I hope what I write will not be off-putting to either Reformed or Arminian (and everything in between) Christians. Though I cannot tackle the complexities of these theological perspectives in this book, I hope this book invites us to common ground for all of us to consider the difficult topics surrounding the unique struggles of life-altering chronic health conditions.

Purpose in Pain

I aim to show there is purpose in our pain because God walks with us in it. We may know some of that purpose in this life, and some we may discover in the next. Before we can discover what purpose of God may be at work through our suffering, we need to come to terms with what we have lost. That may be harder than you realize.

The church in the West has not trained us to lament very well. We have become experts at pretending everything is okay and burying our pain deep inside in the name of faith. As W. Sibley Towner wrote, "We prefer to sin and repent, lament and die in silent privacy."[2] In many sectors of the church, just remaining sick is considered an indictment that your faith is defective. Some have made a virtue of acting like Job's friends. You will find none of that spirit in this book.

While we should always remain open to the possibility of healing this side of the resurrection, this book is for those followers of Jesus who want to deal honestly with what they have lost *if* they are never healed in this life. I do not doubt God's ability to heal me, but his answer has been "Not yet" up to this point. There is nothing wrong with my faith, and certainly, there's nothing wrong with God. It takes a great deal of faith to face up to what is lost and to continue to seek what God will do in our sufferings.

Finally, I write this book because there is a dearth of resources or even acknowledgment of the plight of chronic illness and pain in our churches. That is why I started the Broken and Mended ministry, a nonprofit that exists to connect hurting people to Jesus and each other. I am writing directly to you, the chronic illness and pain sufferer, but I also desire to inspire communities of Christian faith to see those hurting around them. Instead of seeing them as only lost utility, I am inviting pastors and other church leaders to see hurting people as sacred image bearers. God stands with hurting, limited, and disabled people and is ready to show off his perfected strength through weakness (2 Cor 12:9). It's time for churches to stop casting off the ones whom God will use in far more powerful ways than the physical strength they have lost.

So, I invite you to come along for this journey of loss and discovery of renewed purpose. My own journey is reflected in these pages. I believe yours will be, too, in significant ways.

David Heflin
May 2023
Woodward, Oklahoma

2. Peterman and Schmutzer, *Between Pain and Grace*, 103.

Acknowledgments

THOUGH I HAVE PREVIOUSLY published guides for support groups, I have never attempted anything of this scope. I had a few flirtations with book projects, but this one was the first I felt I had to write. That sense of conviction is not usually just a moment of divine inspiration but something formed in the heart through all the ways that God walks with us through sometimes painful journeys. I give thanks to God for his continual faithfulness in working out his purpose for my life. This book is just one of the many outcomes of the ways God has been doing that.

When I began writing this book, I had no idea what an undertaking it would be. When only a chapter or two had been sketched out, my graduate-school professor and now longtime friend, Dr. Sarah Sumner, invited me to a class through her online school, Right On Mission, called simply How to Write a Book. She had no idea that writing a book was exactly what I was undertaking or how much I needed direction at that moment. Dr. Sumner's uncanny sense of timing—it has happened before!—is yet again evidence of God's providential care.

There were many times when my more immediate duties swallowed up months between periods of earnest work on this book. There were long, lonely stages along the way, but writing a book is not a solitary experience. Jeremy Harrison and Esther Smith read drafts of each chapter and provided valuable feedback throughout the process. My wife, Katie, was the first person to read the book in its entirety before I found a publisher. Andrés Ruiz read a later draft and helped me smooth over a few rough edges.

Though I founded Broken and Mended Incorporated, I now answer to its board of directors. They have supported and encouraged me in all areas of my ministry and have empowered me by giving me the time and freedom to invest my creative energies in ways that are mutually beneficial for both Broken and Mended and me. I am grateful for everyone who has served—or is still serving—on the board.

I am also grateful to Wipf and Stock Publishers for giving me the opportunity to share this project with a wider audience. They have helped me fulfill a lifelong dream of writing and publishing a book—made all the better by the purpose of blessing hurting people with the hope of Christ.

For Katie and my children, who are now almost grown, I am deeply thankful. They have faithfully supported me and loved me through everything I have endured. They paid a price as well, and not once did they express resentment for how my struggles affected them; they had only love and concern for my well-being. Thank you always, Josiah, Micah, and Rebekah.

I am grateful for my parents and my siblings, who have always been there for me, and for the many other family members and friends who have stood by me throughout the years. As Clarence tells George Bailey in *It's a Wonderful Life*, "No man is a failure who has friends."[3] By that measure, I have been richly blessed. You know who you are, and I am forever grateful to you.

Finally, I write in this book about a friend I lost in a tragic accident, Chris Blair. Though Chris was not physically present in my life while I wrote this book, his memory and legacy have become a torch of inspiration that I will gladly carry until the end, when we will be reunited by the one who "makes all things new."

3. Capra, *Wonderful Life*, 2:09:40.

Introduction

Purpose Lost

Of Mans First Disobedience, and the Fruit
Of that Forbidden Tree, whose mortal taste
Brought Death into the World, and all our woe,
With loss of Eden, till one greater Man
Restore us, and regain the blissful Seat.

—Opening words to John Milton's *Paradise Lost*[1]

I want to assure you that I have no intention of making this book a pity party for you or me. I don't expect that's why you are reading. You probably don't need any help with that. However, I write from the conviction that in order for us to rediscover purpose in our lives after the onset and persistence of our chronic conditions, we need to lament and grieve what we have lost. It will not serve you well to ignore those realities and quote the often misappropriated passage about how "all things work together for the good" (Rom 8:28).

We will search for the good on this journey, but first, I invite you to a process of lament and grief, grieving what has been lost. Many may wish to avoid that process, but if you do, there's a good

1. Milton, *Paradise Lost*, 1.

chance that rushing ahead to your newfound purpose will eventually result in having to confront that grief anyway, but with much time lost and further disorientation. To get back to paradise, we have to acknowledge how far we are away from it.

You may not have thought of your life as "paradise" even before your health problems started. For some of you, your entire lives have been difficult. How can you lose paradise if you never had it? However, I am not talking about your life as a personal paradise that chronic illness stole from you. None of us have lived in paradise—even if you live in a beautiful place—since Adam and Eve were expelled from the garden of Eden thousands of years ago. That was the paradise that was lost. That's the paradise John Milton wrote about in his epic poem *Paradise Lost.*

With that loss came the struggles and suffering this book will address and that you know all too well in your life. The Bible doesn't start with suffering; it enters with death at the moment humankind rebelled against our Creator. We sense the loss of that paradise, even though we have never lived it personally.

But God's story is not just about what has been lost. It is about an even greater paradise that has been gained through the redemptive work of his son, Jesus. Whatever gains we may experience once we have properly grieved our losses are not because our lives have improved but because through Christ we have already begun participating in his new creation as we become a new creation in Christ ourselves (2 Cor 5:17). So, as we move from Paradise Lost to Paradise Regained in this book, we do so aware that we are participating in a greater story. As our perspective shifts, it does so by recognizing where we are in God's story, even while living under the burden of chronic health conditions.

In the first part of this book, we will survey the sweeping losses that chronic health conditions cause. You may have experienced these losses in part or in whole. The loss of dreams, financial control, time, relationships, dignity, and mental and emotional health is a stark reality that chronic health sufferers experience to varying degrees. Our purpose in this grief is not self-pity but honest reflection and faithful lament. It is only from that perspective that we can eventually say we have regained purpose in our lives and in our walk with God.

In the second part of the book, we will revisit these losses from a different perspective and a deeper reflection on how some losses have led to even greater gains. What Satan intends for evil, God uses for good (Gen 50:20). But we are not ready for that conversation until we have acknowledged what our compromised health has stolen from us. If we are still trying to hold on to our former healthy life, it will be hard to journey forward.

So, first, let's get real about those losses. Let's drop the pretense that everything is fine. We are engaged in a battle that cannot be wȯn without total honesty with ourselves and with God. In the pages that follow, I will share my story and the stories of many others who have walked this difficult road of loss, as we begin to consider what it means to rediscover purpose. Each chapter concludes with reflection questions, offered as an invitation, whether for quiet personal reflection or for shared conversation with others.

Part One

Accepting What Is Lost

Chapter One

The Loss of Dreams

MY CHRONIC ILLNESS STORY

Pain isn't the worst thing that can happen to you—unless it never stops. Many painful experiences become a fading memory if they only last for a little while. But what if the pain doesn't stop? There's a good chance that if you are reading this book, that is no mere hypothetical question. When the pain doesn't stop, then not only does it seem like the worst thing that can happen to you, but it feels like it is the only thing that's happening to you. Pain threatens to become your new defining reality.

Pain mocks purpose and shatters dreams. I've always been a dreamer, and I am often amazed at how differently reality turns out. Had things not happened as they did, would I have still pursued my dreams as originally conceived? I am prone to some pretty wild ideas!

Altered Dreams

It will help to know something about my childhood. Actually, it helps to know something about my mother's childhood first. When Mom was in junior high, she got it in her heart that she wanted a baby boy named David one day. I don't know if she was inspired by Hannah's prayer or not, but Mom promised that if God answered her prayer, she would dedicate him to the Lord. She meant she would raise her son to be a preacher. Thanks, Mom! I never had a chance!

However, I wasn't always keen on being a preacher or in ministry at all. For a brief time in middle school, shortly after I decided to follow Jesus, I was amenable to the idea, but it wasn't the only thing I was interested in. Inspired by the original *Karate Kid* movies, my brother and I joined a taekwondo studio. We took it as seriously as a ten-year-old and a seven-year-old could take it. Once my dad got into the action, our home became an extension of our school. Mom thought we were going to knock over our single-wide home! She eventually gave in, too, and I taught her all the way through her green belt.

I did well in instructing my mom and other students. Still others thought I should go into ministry. The solution? I decided I was going to be a taekwondo instructor *and* a preacher! This always brought a chuckle from the older, polite members of my childhood church. However, as I reached high school, becoming a preacher was the furthest thing from my mind, and my interest in martial arts was waning, too.

By the time I was sixteen, I was one rank below black belt, but girls and football became more important to me, and if I'm being honest, I was intimidated by the prospect of the black belt test. I became less involved in taekwondo and eventually dropped out. Later, I considered it my biggest childhood regret.

My regrets multiplied as I became an older high school student and then a college student at Sam Houston State University. My faith was less important to me than the latest party. My aim was popularity with my friends and the attention of the young women around me.

I originally majored in criminal justice, intending to become a Texas state trooper after college. However, my academic focus diminished to the point that I lost my eligibility for financial aid. I was broke until my eligibility was restored in the second semester of my sophomore year, which I then followed up with three Fs and a D. Not surprisingly, it turned out to be my last semester at Sam Houston.

Recently, I was invited to speak at both of my sons' baccalaureate services (2022 and 2024, respectively). As I looked out over the crowd full of seniors and their families, I thought to myself, "If they only knew what kind of student I was, they would definitely choose another speaker!" However, I could also tell them that when life doesn't go as you expect, that does not mean it is the end of your story. Mine was just beginning.

I am not proud of any of these academic and spiritual failures, but it was not all for loss. Early on in my last semester at Sam Houston, my parents received an invitation to a dinner from the campus ministry I was supposedly involved in. Not wanting my parents to know the full extent of my rebellion, I went to the dinner with them. All was going according to plan when a member of the campus ministry walked up to my parents and introduced himself as Jean (pronounced like Shawn). Then he looked at me and told my parents, "Oh, I've never seen him before!" I was busted!

Jean and I became such good friends that we were later roommates and the best man in each other's weddings. It was the first step among many to my spiritual recovery. Jean was the first of a combination of people that God put in my life at just the right time, and I experienced a God who pursued me with his great love even when I was at my worst. I was like Jonah, who had been on the run from God, but I did not really know the God I was running from. The word of God was burning in my heart while I read Romans at my graveyard shift at a juvenile detention center. Part of the reason I struggled so much academically was because of that graveyard shift five days a week. I wouldn't trade it for anything, however, as the kids I was responsible for slept through the night. I spent hours in God's word, riveted in a way I had never been before.

Earlier that semester, I became convinced that if Jesus really rose from the dead, then there could be nothing or no one more important in life. God called my bluff. He showed himself to me in so many ways that I would have to be a willing fool to keep denying him. So, one night I was walking underneath the trees of a moonlit state park in Huntsville, Texas. Somewhere along that walk, I fell to my knees in surrender to the risen Lord, and I told him I would do whatever he wanted me to do. During this time, I profoundly experienced the call to ministry.

It isn't important right now to tell in detail what happened in the ensuing years. I eventually ended up as the preaching minister in Palm Springs, California, in 2004, nine years after that fateful night in the park. Later, we moved on to Portales, New Mexico, in the same role in 2010. Mom got her prayers answered after all. Unexpectedly, martial arts was about to reenter my life as well.

We had an eighth-degree black belt in Portales, who taught taekwondo at affordable rates for families. I enrolled with my seven-year-old son. My five-year-old son joined a little later. I started as a white belt, but I was so excited to be back in martial arts, and I was pleasantly surprised by how quickly the skills and moves came back to me. I was not your ordinary white belt. Muscle memory can be an amazing thing!

However, one thing didn't come back so easily: flexibility. I did not expect to be able to drop down into the splits like I could in high school, but my hips felt exceptionally tight. I couldn't know it at the time, but the tightness in my hips was a harbinger of trouble, and it was beyond normal out-of-shape inflexibility. One of the stretches we did frequently—called butterflies—required us to bring our feet together with our knees facing out. Then you pushed down on the inside of your legs with your elbows so that your knees came nearer to the floor. My knees hardly moved at all, and my hips always felt as tight the next time I stretched them.

I did what any stubborn thirty-something-year-old dad would do; I ignored it. I had started running as well, getting in shape for taekwondo, while also training for a local ten-kilometer race. I eventually dropped forty pounds of extra weight. Everything was going great except for the flexibility issues in my hips. My enthusiasm was not daunted. I believed in a few short years that I would reverse my childhood regret and get my black belt.

Back to those wild dreams! I envisioned myself becoming an instructor, moving to a bigger city, and opening my own taekwondo school. I did not want to give up ministry, either. So, as if God were bringing those childhood aspirations full circle, I imagined a future where my passion for martial arts and my calling to ministry would finally belong together. Little did I know that half of that dream would soon become impossible, and it took a while for me to understand and accept that. Recently, I accidentally came across a document on my computer that I had entitled "Church Plant: Theology and Plan." It was a painful reminder of the plan that never happened.

In March of 2011, as I was doing kicking drills across the studio floor, I felt a sharp pain in my left hip, the hip I was pivoting on to do a sidekick. Two days later, I felt the same sensation in my right hip. I thought I had pulled or strained muscles in both my hips, so I tried to protect them by not kicking so high and putting too much pressure on the back leg, but no matter what I did, the pain kept getting worse.

I ran my ten-kilometer race in June with little trouble. I could run because I didn't have to twist my hips like I did with kicking, but I decided to shut it down after the race, and I counted on healing up by August when the taekwondo lessons resumed (our school was closed in the summer months). On the first day that I warmed up on my own, I knew there was trouble. It felt like I hadn't rested my hips for a single day. They hurt just as badly as they had before I had shut down my workouts.

At this point, I need to sum up briefly what happened over the next nine months or so. I tried to continue taekwondo. During this time, I participated in my first tournament since I was a kid. It turned out there was only one other participant in my age group, so the odds weren't bad, except for one problem: I could barely kick above the waist of an average-sized man, and my opponent was six feet five! But at least I got second place!

Everyone was giving me advice, all of it unhelpful. One doctor told me, "I didn't do sickness very well." Another suggested it was all in my head when I didn't respond well to his at-home exercises. I tried the chiropractor, too. My hips only got worse. I finished my last belt test in December of 2011. The one critique I received was that I was not kicking high enough. Like in the tournament just a few months prior, at most, I could kick straight out but could not raise my legs past the level of my hips, and even that was extremely painful.

Finally, two orthopedic surgeons diagnosed me with hip impingement and labral tears in both hips. This meant the ball and socket of my hip joint had extra bone growth, so that when I was rotating on my hips, that extra bone was cutting into my hip labrum every time. While this diagnosis wasn't great news, at least I knew. I believed arthroscopic hip surgeries would repair my hips, and then I would be on the path to recovery. However, before the surgery ever took place, I heard my surgeon say while looking at my x-rays, "Something's not right."

He was looking at the lost space in my SI joints in my lower back. It was the first time I heard the words "ankylosing spondylitis," but it would not be the last. After surgery on my left hip in May of 2012, I struggled to recover. My new rheumatologist quickly confirmed my surgeon's suspicion in August of that same year. I had an autoimmune disease that caused my immune system to attack healthy joints and tissue throughout my body, which, among other things, caused extra bone growth, such as what I had experienced in my hips. My doctor believed we caught it early and immediately wanted me to start Enbrel, a weekly pen injection that is a powerful immunosuppressant drug. It was all moving too fast for me and in the wrong direction.

Enbrel helped a little for a while, but a whole new set of problems started in 2013. It began on an anniversary getaway with my wife. At first, I thought the painful cramping and diarrhea would pass like a bug or some food that didn't agree with me, but when we got home, it just got worse. I vividly remember lying on my bathroom floor in agony, praying for relief. A short time after that, I began to have problems swallowing food, and I found myself with yet another doctor, a gastroenterologist (GI).

Along with all the other usual tests a GI does, he also ordered a liver biopsy due to continued elevated liver enzymes. This brought even more bad news. I had stage two fibrosis of the liver. Stage four is cirrhosis. My GI found eosinophils in my colon (a very rare condition called eosinophilic colitis) and the same in my esophagus, which had significant tissue damage. He began to believe that my underlying problem was not ankylosing spondylitis but a more dangerous and potential threat to my liver: eosinophilia. He referred me to the Mayo Clinic.

My wife, Katie, and I could not keep up with all this news emotionally. Every doctor's appointment or new test brought down waves of disorientation on our heads. Confusion and disbelief were common occurrences. Before my November trip to Mayo in Rochester, Minnesota, I remember driving in our adopted hometown of Portales, New Mexico, one late fall afternoon, and the song "Worn" by Tenth Avenue North came on the radio. That song (and the official video as well) is a true modern-day lament. The title is descriptive of those moments where we have nothing left. The song looks for redemption, but it doesn't rush past the agony and grief. Its path to hope is not around grief but through it. "Worn" still ministers to me on bad days. As we listened to that song, our eyes filled with tears. Would I need a liver transplant? Was it really possible that my life was in danger?

For the most part, Katie didn't go there, but my mind naturally gravitates toward the big-picture questions. Here I was, a husband and father of three, still just thirty-seven years old, and still struggling to recover from a hip surgery that was eighteen months in the past. It had been thirty months since the hip injuries, and my life had constantly gotten worse.

I have yet to mention that we had adopted an individual health insurance policy for me that was intended for emergency use. After all, I had no significant health problems when we made that decision. When the Mayo trip came, my wife had just gone back to work a couple of months prior, and she was able to get me on her group plan. However, the financial debt was already piling up by the thousands. Mayo was going to put us back another two grand.

These are the hidden realities of chronic illnesses, injuries, and pain. It isn't just inconvenient; it's life-altering. My entire future was clouded. Becoming a black belt? Starting a taekwondo school? Planting a church? That version of my life was not only canceled; it was eradicated. The sparring gear and sports bag I used to carry to taekwondo class stayed buried in the closet until we could finally give them away—a final admission that my life was not going back to the way it was. We all had different dreams when chronic pain, illness, or disability struck. Those dreams fueled our lives with purpose, a purpose that has been lost.

Finding a New Normal

We were greatly relieved to discover while at the Mayo Clinic that my situation was not as dire as we had feared. If there has been healing on my journey, it happened then. A lot of people were praying for me. I had started some new medications, but what happened at Mayo was completely unexpected. My original biopsies were confirmed, but after repeating the scopes, no eosinophils were found where they weren't supposed to be. My blood work and all my tests came back better than they had been in months! At the time, I found this confusing. Did we go to Mayo for no reason? No one could explain why the biopsies in Texas came back with eosinophils and why the ones in Minnesota did not.

In 2023, I had an MRI done on my liver with results declaring that the significant liver damage from 2013 was long gone. Just like with the biopsies, I didn't understand the dramatic change from a medical standpoint. My esophagus had healed as well. Nothing really makes sense, but what makes the *most* sense to me is that God intervened.

The first GI was not wrong. I simply did not have the same condition at Mayo that I had before I went there, but I never considered it a "healing" until recently. It was more like dodging a bullet. Today, I believe that God healed me in the shadow of these other chronic conditions, with which I still live. Even when we don't get the complete healing we pray for, that doesn't mean we can't experience partial healing along the way or be spared from a grimmer diagnosis. But some well-meaning people in your life won't be satisfied with these partial healings. For them, it is all or nothing! However, Scripture never promises that every healing will be total or immediate.

We should celebrate every healing from God, big or small. In my case, God did not deliver me from the long, hard road of chronic illness, but he did spare me from a more dangerous outcome. I haven't gone back to Mayo. I have no plans to return. Of course, things could change for me, as they could for you. If and when they do, let's remember that God's healing can come in many unexpected ways, even under the shadows of our chronic conditions. At the Mayo Clinic, I met with a top-notch gastroenterologist, a rheumatologist, and an allergist, but instead of diagnosing me with eosinophilia, they concluded I had Crohn's disease, as well as confirmed my prior diagnosis of ankylosing spondylitis.

My GI in Amarillo was not satisfied with the Crohn's diagnosis. He was convinced he was right about eosinophilia being the main culprit. He may have been right, but the problems that sent me to Mayo never returned. God answered many prayers on my behalf, and the more serious implications of my autoimmune issues were divinely removed. Or, at least, that's what I believe happened. However, Crohn's and ankylosing spondylitis still meant many difficult days ahead.

After Mayo, my chronic pain symptoms were mostly under control, and despite the bleaker financial situation, we entered into a new normal. I was grateful that the pain was mostly mild and my gastrointestinal symptoms were held in check. I went about the business of living with plenty to do. After some struggles unrelated to my health problems, circumstances were improving at the church where I worked. My growing kids took most of the rest of my time. I even got involved in coaching them in football. Life wasn't so bad.

We need seasons of life when we get used to a new normal, though I know not everyone gets that opportunity. Even in this calmer season, the truth remained that my dreams were still long gone. There would be no resurgence of an athletic life as I approached my forties. I was never all that athletic anyway, but that doesn't mean I didn't enjoy trying!

Maybe you were already living the dream. A good friend of mine had to give up his career as a band teacher because of ankylosing spondylitis. He was doing what he loved. It crushed him to relinquish his career, but eventually he came to terms with his loss and established a new normal.

I am convinced that we have to accept our losses before we can ever discover the hard-earned gains that come from chronic illness and pain. If we don't reach this point of acceptance, we will get stuck in limbo between our lost dreams and a new potential normal. If you are already languishing in that limbo, my hope is that this book will help you spring free.

It is understandable to spend a season of life adapting to a new normal while not quite letting go of that old normal. What if a medicine or other medical treatment allows you to gain back some of what you have lost? Maybe things progressed so badly before proper diagnosis and treatment, but now, you are in a season of regaining what you thought was gone. No one can discern these periods of life better than you and your loved ones with God's help.

GOD'S ENDURING CALL

Sometimes, even after medical intervention, you might not get better, let alone return to your previous healthy condition. To accept that the life you once pursued and loved has been irretrievably lost breaks your spirit. It is certainly reasonable to need some time before accepting a drastic new reality. Linger here, but don't get stuck here. How can you begin life again walking down a new path that you never wanted?

It may help to realize that the idea of making your identity about pursuing the desires of your heart is not a universal expectation but rather one that is encouraged primarily in the West. I've spent some time listening to the Bema Podcast,[1] a journey through the Bible with Marty Solomon, a Jewish believer. He opened my eyes to this reality when he talked about the magnitude of Abraham leaving his father behind to follow the call of God (Gen 12:1–3). In the ancient Near East—and in many cultures today—destinies were not tied to aptitude tests and personal passions. You

1. Solomon, "Letting Go."

didn't follow your heart. Your destiny was tied directly to your father's house. Sons learned to do what their fathers did. Daughters learned from their mothers. Sons and daughters did not just set out on their own to follow their dreams.

Their way isn't necessarily better than our way. It is just an example of how God is not tied to a particular way of doing things. Therefore, his call on your life did not end just because your dreams got upended. Calling is anchored in God's initiative, not in our plans unfolding how we envisioned them. And this is critical to embrace if we are going to accept a new reality, one that we did not choose. Aren and Trina Bahadourian share their story often to help others forced into a new and painful reality hold on to hope.

I interviewed Aren and Trina for Broken and Mended's podcast, *In The Seams*.[2] After finally adjusting to Trina's life-altering diagnosis of chronic Lyme disease, they began a ministry called Remain to help people *remain* in Christ throughout their suffering. Unfortunately, their personal suffering was just beginning.

When Trina was pregnant with their third son, they received devastating news that their son, diagnosed with trisomy 13, would not live but a few hours at most after he was born. They made it clear to their medical providers, friends, and family that abortion was not an option; they would not even mention the term. They prayed for a miracle and stepped forward into their unknown future by naming their son Isaiah Orion, or Ori for short. I wish I could tell you that they got their miracle and that Ori is living a long and healthy life, but sadly, his life ended three hours after he was born. What does the world see in a story like that? Wasted? Useless? Should they have given up and had an abortion?

But Trina heard a different voice and believed God was asking her, "Do you trust me to write him a different story?" Through the eyes of faith, we see that Ori's story is not over. This life is only a prelude to eternity. And Ori lives in the arms of God, and his story is touching lives around the world as his parents share their pain and their hope with others who face similar trials.

2. Heflin, "Interview with Remain Founders."

It's not the story the Bahadourians would have chosen. You may be reckoning with the reality that you are living a story you did not choose. There's nothing wrong with acknowledging that. In fact, we must come to terms with what we have lost due to our chronic health conditions. However, the question Trina heard God say in her heart haunts me with this slight adaptation, "Do you trust me to write *you* a different story?"

We didn't sign up to follow Jesus because we believed we were the most qualified authors to write our story. We decided to follow Jesus because we had already tried writing our own stories and realized it is a disaster unless God holds the pen. Sometimes the story unfolds like we want. Sometimes it unfolds in the opposite direction of what we want. But the question remains, "Do you trust me to write you a different story?" But to lean into the story that God is calling us into, we need to learn how to lament the one we had to give up.

LEARNING LAMENT

It is wise and healthy to lament the loss of your dreams. However, our church culture in the West doesn't encourage this, especially among Protestants. From the early days of the Protestant Reformation, Timothy Keller wrote, "Christians were taught not to weep or cry but to show God their faith through unflinching, joyful acceptance of his will."[3] Even if you were not aware of this, you can notice it in the songs we sing. Look at the lyrics of most modern worship songs and you will be hard-pressed to find more than a few songs that could be classified as lament, which is strange since lament makes up 40 percent of the church's first hymn book, the Psalms.[4]

Not only do we have an aversion to lament, but we also specialize in diversion. One of the reasons I believe that Broken and Mended took off in East Africa so much faster than it did in the United States is that the majority of Africans do not have access to

3. Keller, *Walking with God*, 241.

4. Pemberton, *Hurting with God*, 65.

thousands of hours of mind-numbing streaming programs. They had room in their hearts and schedules for support groups because they were desperate for spiritual encouragement. They were also not afraid of lament because they knew how much they needed to cry out to God. He is their only refuge.

Too often, instead of facing our troubles with honesty, we drown them with distraction. This is too much like numbing the pain of a dangerous injury. We may feel the pain less, but our wounds only get worse. Becoming reacquainted with the ancient practice of lament is the remedy we need in our private devotions and corporate worship settings. Lament helps us to reckon honestly with our upended life so we can one day move forward.

Perhaps you believed you were following God's exact plan for your life just like Bethany. Bethany grew up as a child of Bible translators in Nairobi. From an early age, she knew she was called to do missionary work. She married a preacher in college, who was happily on board with this plan. In fact, Jared was studying to be a Bible translator. It was as if God blessed her with the perfect mate for what she was called to do. Bethany completed a nursing degree to open up opportunities in the mission field. Everything was on track.

As Bethany and Jared were making preparations, their first child entered their lives. She had a difficult pregnancy, and after giving birth, she experienced significant pain and fatigue. Eventually, she was diagnosed with a connective tissue disorder called Ehlers-Danlos syndrome.

Her suffering reached the point that Bethany had to quit her job. Her first child also had a congenital defect. Suddenly, missionary dreams had to be put on hold, and sometimes dreams put on hold never get revived, especially when it becomes apparent that the pain and fatigue aren't going anywhere. Even when Bethany found a new purpose as a transplant coordinator, she was not able to keep her job when her conditions worsened again. She shared her story on Broken and Mended's podcast, *In The Seams*:

> Because one of the responsibilities of a transplant coordinator is to be on call. And to be on call, I could be up,

> you know, all weekend long and then expected to be back in the office, and I couldn't do it anymore. It was just too much. That was probably the hardest transition for me because I felt like I had finally found the place where the Lord wanted me and the place where I could serve, in addition to being able to care for my family. But I couldn't do it anymore. And the symptoms and the health issues, I felt like had taken that away from me.[5]

Bethany felt like God had let her down. Why wouldn't God want her to be a missionary? Why did she feel such a yearning for missions if her health prevented her from pursuing her calling? And why, when she had finally accepted the loss of one dream and found another as a transplant coordinator, was her dream taken away again? These are hard questions without any certain answers, but her story did not end in disillusionment. We will come back to Bethany's story in chapter 7.

If you have a lost life dream because of your own journey with chronic illness, you might feel let down by God, like Bethany did. You are not alone. Many faithful worshipers of God have recorded their laments in the Psalms. "My God, my God, why have you forsaken me?" (Ps 22:1) was not spontaneously composed by Jesus on the cross but had been cried out for generations by those who felt abandoned by God during their crises. Their laments often expressed a communal cry more than the loss of individual aspirations. Consider a psalm of Asaph written to a devastated people living in exile:

> O God, pagan nations have conquered your land,
> your special possession.
> They have defiled your holy Temple
> and made Jerusalem a heap of ruins.
> They have left the bodies of your servants
> as food for the birds of heaven.
> The flesh of your godly ones
> has become food for the wild animals.
> Blood has flowed like water all around Jerusalem;
> no one is left to bury the dead.

5. Heflin, "Chronic Illness."

We are mocked by our neighbors,
an object of scorn and derision to those around us.
O Lord, how long will you be angry with us? Forever?
How long will your jealousy burn like fire? (Ps 79:1–5 NLT)

The exilic Israelites' loss of their temple, holy city, and tribal homeland is not relatable for people living in Western society today, though the people of Ukraine could relate on a level most of us could never reach. This is what it means to be the people of God and find yourself sitting on the rubble of lost dreams. When they lamented, they were not unfaithful. They were crying out to the only one who could redeem them. This is the proper context by which to understand the oft-quoted passage of Jer 29:11: "'For I know the plans I have for you,' says the Lord. 'They are plans for good and not for disaster, to give you a future and a hope.'" God's steadfast love is so far-reaching that even the ruinous loss of a homeland could not destroy their purpose in God. Lament provided a framework for faithfully expressing the depths of their losses while they awaited their faithful God's redemption.

Whether lamenting what is lost as a community or for a more personal tragedy, our aim is to hope in our Creator. When we truly hope in God, we are no longer consumed by perishable and passing things. Our health struggles remind us of the brevity of our lives and teach us that we are not in control, but God is. This is not a bad thing to be reminded of. The psalmist even asks God to remind him of this truth:

Lord, make me aware of my end
and the number of my days
so that I will know how short-lived I am.
In fact, you have made my days just inches long,
and my life span is as nothing to you.
Yes, every human being stands as only a vapor. *Selah*
Yes, a person goes about like a mere shadow.
Indeed, they rush around in vain,
gathering possessions
without knowing who will get them.
Now, Lord, what do I wait for?
My hope is in you. (Ps 39:4–7)

When we lose our dreams, we lose our illusions of control. Do not think yourself poorer for that discovery. For it was always an illusion, even when you thought otherwise. Chronic illness and pain remap the journey we thought we were on and deliver us from the false belief that we are in control of our own lives. Many of your healthy friends and family are still under the illusion from which you have been delivered. Lament your losses for sure, but remember this: you were never in control, even before you got sick or hurt. Remembering this will re-center and revive your hope. The one in whom we hope is never surprised by anything, and that is hope to hold on to when your life is spinning out of control.

REFLECTION QUESTIONS

1. In what ways have you experienced God's healing—physical, emotional, or spiritual—on your chronic illness journey?
2. How would you describe your "new normal," and what has been most difficult or most life-giving about it?
3. In what ways does our modern view of "pursuing your dreams" differ from how people in biblical times understood purpose and calling?
4. How difficult is it for you to trust God to write a different story for your life than the one you envisioned? What makes that trust easier or harder?
5. How can lamenting your lost dreams help you move forward in life today?

Chapter Two

The Loss of Financial Control

TALKING ABOUT MONEY

In the fall of 2009, before my chronic health issues began, I was interviewed on the phone for an open ministry position. The church leaders on the other end of the line began peppering me with questions about my financial circumstances. They were especially concerned about how much debt we carried. It became clear that part of their assessment of me as a candidate was my financial status, but the context did not matter. If you had debt, you were obviously an undisciplined and irresponsible person. I did not continue with the interview process.

My reluctance to talk about my finances with total strangers is on par with how most of us feel about divulging our financial circumstances to others. We tend to be very private about money. As a consequence, many people have no idea how devastating chronic illnesses and other chronic health conditions can be on sufferers and their families. Many sufferers don't want to share because they believe they will be judged for their struggles or because others just do not want to hear it.

I made the decision to be open about our financial journey, not because it is cathartic, but because I know it is important for people to be informed that financial crises caused by chronic health conditions are no small issue. More importantly, I want you to know that if you share a similar journey, you are not alone. We are on this journey together, and we can still find hope and encouragement from one another when we share our stories. So, let me begin with my personal story.

MY FINANCIAL CRISIS STORY

Before I knew anything about ankylosing spondylitis, Crohn's, or the Mayo Clinic, I needed an MRI to discover why my hips were ailing. It was going to cost us $1,000. We did not have any kind of savings account, and it would have taken us a good while to save that amount of money. We would have to absorb it as debt.

We were already carrying a lot of debt from school loans, medical debt related to my wife's first pregnancy, and a brief but costly venture as landlords. It seemed like we were finally making progress, and I struggled to submit myself to a procedure that would set us back. Katie persuaded me that I would not hesitate if it were her or one of the kids who needed it. So, we got the MRI and hoped that would be the worst of it.

You would not be reading this book had that been the worst of it. It was the beginning of such overwhelming financial demands that we eventually became numb to the waves of medical bills that came crashing down on us. Our mailbox was stuffed with EOBs (Explanation of Benefits). We piled them on our counter knowing they never contained any good news. The portion the patient was expected to pay was just more wood on a fire that we could never put out.

Between 2011 and 2013, we amassed over $30,000 in out-of-pocket expenses, not counting insurance premiums. Had it not been for some very generous friends who loaned us money interest-free with a pay-as-you-can plan, we likely would have declared bankruptcy. We had already gone through foreclosure when I was laid off in 2009 during the housing market crash. We did not want bankruptcy in our history as well. For over a decade, we somehow managed to pay our bills, but that is no longer true. We have avoided bankruptcy, but everything is difficult due to our medical bills.

We are very grateful for those generous friends. They could not have respected our dignity any more than they did in offering to help, but even with people like them, it is hard to shake the feeling of failure when you need that level of help just to survive. I know that needing help should not be shame-inducing, but I felt the emotional tension nonetheless. I know many of you likely do as well. It is always gut-wrenching to have to explain to our kids, yet again, why we don't have any money like so many of our healthy friends. Whenever we did have an increase in income, it just meant more money to throw at an overwhelming pile of debt. It is hard not to feel shame when you feel like you never have enough. We will delve deeper into the experiences of shame and how Scripture addresses it in later chapters. For now, I want to keep the focus on the direct fallout from mounting medical expenses, which can be, and often is, devastating.

My story is not unique, and if you experienced financial pain and loss due to chronic illness, neither is yours. Ninety percent of the nation's $4.5 trillion in yearly medical spending is for chronic physical and mental health conditions.[1] Many are forced to default on major financial obligations. They struggle to see their peers with similar incomes enjoy life with the financial margin they will never have, all the while knowing that their next medical bill may be the one they just cannot absorb. This scenario assumes they have been able to keep their jobs. Unfortunately, that is not always the case. Many chronically ill people, like my friend RaeDeen, are forced to abandon their careers or greatly reduce their workload.

STORIES FROM OTHERS

RaeDeen worked in middle management for the largest charitable trust fund in Hawaii for the benefit of school children. Her job required a lot of travel from Hawaii to the mainland and unapologetically demanded long hours. RaeDeen was already living with chronic health conditions and could have filed for disability, but she wanted to work. However, the price became too heavy, and

1. Centers for Disease Control and Prevention, "Fast Facts."

to survive, RaeDeen requested accommodations, including being released from all "non-essential travel."

RaeDeen describes the working environment in this large trust fund organization as "very corporate" and "very toxic." They retaliated against her for asking for accommodations. They made her job even more demanding. "I had to kill myself to make money," she said. She feared walking away because she needed the medical insurance. She knew she could not survive such a demanding job, and she filed a complaint with the Equal Employment Opportunity Commission and was placed on a ten-month administrative leave. Later, she withdrew that complaint to protect her coworkers. Her company rewarded her by firing her.

As she searched for new jobs with less demanding expectations, she discovered that she had been blackballed because of the vindictiveness of her former employer. Her financial situation became "terrifying," and she almost sold her home to survive. RaeDeen's chronic illness, and her employer's reaction to it, cost RaeDeen her job, her work, her reputation, and her home. She still had to find a way to get health insurance. She was facing $900 monthly premiums as a self-employed worker, not to mention thousands of dollars in co-payments.

Financial struggle is often another unseen crisis impacting families dealing with chronic illness. In fact, it is likely a safe assumption that your friends, neighbors, church members, or family members who have prolonged medical issues have considerable financial struggles as well. These financial struggles are life-altering in themselves, not to mention the pain and fatigue of illness and injury.

Even with good insurance policies, you may be paying an enormous amount for co-pays for doctors' visits and prescriptions, deductibles, and out-of-pocket maximums. In my own situation, I usually meet my out-of-pocket maximum in the first quarter of the year! And it's not like no one else in the family ever has medical costs. Since the birth of my children, there have been seven other surgeries for other family members. All three of my kids needed braces. They all needed corrective lenses. And none of this means they want a car less than their friends when that time comes!

My point is not to ask for your pity. Most likely you have experienced a comparable situation. My point is to acknowledge how much more difficult chronic illness has made your life financially and to alleviate the guilt that you might be experiencing because you feel like you have put your family in a difficult situation.

An added difficulty for us is that we have lived far away from both of our families. It wasn't just an option not to travel because we did not have the money if we wanted to see our families. We kept up these visits the best we could, but there was always a steep cost. If you have a lot of margin in your budget, this tension between traveling to see family or staying home to avoid debt might not make much sense to you, but many of you can relate to what I am describing.

I have talked to many other people, like Gail, who can relate to this struggle when the cost exceeds the capacity to travel at all. Gail told me about vacations never taken, causes they couldn't give to, and her husband having to work well past his retirement age because of the financial strain of her chronic illness. The financial implications can impact what we have to leave behind, if anything is left. From the onset of medical treatment to the grave, the financial consequences stick around like bugs on a windshield with nothing to scrape them off! Of course, the degree of this impact varies according to factors like insurance coverage, the viability of a career after the illness/injury, resources available from family, the cost of medical treatment, and so on. Amy is one of the more extreme cases I know of.

After she had COVID-19, her life as she knew it came to a halt. She could not leave her bedroom, let alone go back to work as a teacher. Her husband was still able to work, but one-third of his paycheck went to Amy's monthly care. They started with two full-time jobs and now had two-thirds of one salary left to live on. But as Amy's mysterious illness continued to worsen, she needed aggressive medical treatment in Barcelona, Spain (Amy lives in Utah). Amy's family needed to raise $140,000 to pay for this medical care! They crowdfunded to get her to Barcelona, but the total cost for this necessary care may hound them for the rest of their lives.

We each have our own financial story, but no matter how bad it gets, we need to remember we are not alone. Financial crises caused by chronic health conditions are life-changers, but they need not define the totality of our lives. I will have more to say about that in chapter 9, including wisdom shared by some of the people in the stories above.

This part of the book is about acknowledging our losses so we can better take hold of our gains, but the gains must wait for now. In the face of such overwhelming financial pressure, Scripture gives us language for expressing our deep losses and anxious concerns about the future. I again turn to the Psalms: "But as for me, I am poor and needy; may the Lord think of me. You are my help and my deliverer; you are my God, do not delay" (Ps 40:17 NIV).

LESSONS FROM A SHEPHERD ON THE RUN

This psalm is attributed to David. We are not accustomed to thinking of kings as poor and needy. Yet David was not always a king. He was the youngest son of eight brothers and was a humble shepherd who had to defend his sheep at the risk of his life. David fled from his predecessor, Saul, for years and lived as an exile dependent on the hospitality of Israel's enemies. David knew what it meant to be poor and needy, a lesson he was forced to learn again when he had to flee from his own son, Absalom.

David's psalms are full of imprecations against his very real enemies, but David's greatest legacy—the reason I believe he was called a man after God's own heart—is that he always knew whom to cry out to for help. David was a deeply flawed man, but he was not an idolater. His trust remained in his Lord through it all. His psalms become a template for our cries as well.

Like the apostle Paul would later say about himself (Phil 4:12), David knew what it was to be in want and to have plenty. He knew how quickly a favorable situation could be reversed. David knew the meaning of depending on God for deliverance because he had no one else who could help him.

That same delivering God is here for us in our financial crises. You may not know when, or even if, financial relief will come to you, but you can decide today to cry out to God in your need. You can let God sustain you in a time of want, and you can know that the God who sees is the same God who provides.[2]

REFLECTION QUESTIONS

1. How have your chronic health conditions changed the way you think about money or financial security?
2. Is it hard for you to ask for or receive help from others? Why do you think that is?
3. Which story or example in this chapter did you relate to the most, and why?
4. Why do you think the author chose David as a "template for our cries"? What stands out to you about his example?
5. How has your financial situation—whether tight or uncertain—affected your relationship with God?

2. Hartley, *Genesis*, 208.

Chapter Three

The Loss of Time

I fled, and cry'd out DEATH;
Hell trembl'd at the hideous
Name, and sigh'd
From all her Caves, and back resounded DEATH.
I fled, but he pursued.

—SIN RECOUNTING THE MOMENT SHE NAMED HER OFFSPRING DEATH, *PARADISE LOST*[1]

WHAT MAKES TIME COUNT

Milton's poem vividly personifies Sin giving birth to her child, Death—a grotesque image meant to show that even sin cannot escape the power of death once it enters the world. With death's inevitable approach, time becomes relevant in a new and frightening way, but time is not the problem if there is no death. Death has always been and still is our greatest enemy.

A wise professor once asked our graduate theology class what was the world's greatest problem. Each of us offered our best guess as to what she was looking for. Some said disease. Others

1. Milton, *Paradise Lost*, 50.

said crime or poverty. A few came closer to the mark by suggesting sin. But none of us answered, "Death." The professor leaped at the teaching moment. The one common woe that everyone in the world shares is death. Religions and worldviews conflict with virtually every other truth claim, but no one can reasonably deny that we are all going to die.

Death makes time count. We measure this precious resource against a ticking clock that is counting down the span of our lives. I don't mean to be morbid, but our awareness of death's approach highlights the value of the time each of us has. This is why we care when other intruders—like chronic illness—deprive us of time.

You have likely had the experience of someone saying to you, "This week has really flown by," while your experience made it seem like it crawled by. While time itself is an objective reality, we experience it subjectively. I point this out because one of my readers of an early version of this chapter, Esther Smith, didn't connect well with how I described my experience. I felt like time was slipping by, and I was losing the time for the things that matter to me. Esther, however, felt like time stood still. It was as if all of a sudden, she had a ton of time, but no physical capacity to do anything with it. I remember that her website and Facebook group for people with chronic illness used to be called Life in Slow Motion, an apt description of Esther's (and many others') experience of time while living with chronic illness.

So, whether chronic illness and pain have caused you to experience time as slipping away or as standing still, the main point is that these chronic health conditions warp our experience of time. Maybe chronic illness has crowded your already busy calendar with doctors' appointments or other medically related endeavors. Or maybe you have a disability that causes you to experience time as a surplus but with no way to fill it. However we process that time warp, we recognize that our time is not our own in the way we thought it was before illness and chronic pain. In this chapter, we will wrestle with this time-robbing invader and how to face up to the world's greatest problem that we would all rather avoid.

THE TICKING CLOCK

Depictions of time in literature or film are almost always a countdown to a catastrophic fate. Charles Dickens hauntingly describes a condemned man's last day as he hears the chime of the bell at each hour in *A Tale of Two Cities*.[2] Perhaps better known—thanks to many great adaptations—is the chiming of the clock at either one or two o'clock in the morning as each ghost visits Ebenezer Scrooge in *A Christmas Carol*.[3] The Wicked Witch's hourglass in *The Wizard of Oz*[4] or the frightening gonging of the more recent example of the grandfather clock in Netflix's *Stranger Things* showcase time as the approaching doom of death.[5] These depictions work because they accurately reflect our unease with time. "Time stands still for no one," we exclaim.

Yet it is for that reason we treasure time as a precious resource. None of us has an unlimited amount of it. None of us knows exactly how much we have. We are anxious while sitting at a stoplight or standing in line inside the grocery store because we can't shake the unnerving feeling that we are wasting time. Once time is gone, it is gone forever. If chronic illness and pain threaten to steal time from us, then it is a threat that strikes a vicious blow to a resource that is second only to life itself.

In my town, a church puts on the same play every year. The premise is that people are living carefree lives with little to no thought about their personal expiring clock. Each of the characters is met with an unexpected demise and then wakes up in their eternal home, heaven or hell, based on their preparedness for their death. Whatever their eternal fate, what the characters have in common is that they all had less time than they realized.

I am not a fan of trying to scare people into conversion, but I assume these tactics are effective because they keep performing the play. When you cause someone to slow down to think about

2. Dickens, *Tale of Two Cities*, 340–45.
3. Dickens, *Christmas Carol*, 37–41, 71–76.
4. Fleming, *Wizard of Oz*, 123:42.
5. Duffer and Duffer, *Stranger Things*, season 4.

the unknown quantity of his or her life, it has an impact. It points out our mortality in an uncomfortable way. Chronic illnesses and pain do this with startling clarity. Tick. Tock.

HOW PAIN ROBS YOUR TIME

Your pain does not have to be chronic for you to experience a considerable loss of time. An injury takes time to dress and nurse back to health. Athletes lose entire seasons to injuries that require surgery and rehab. Every person who has lived through childhood knows how sickness can abruptly halt life. But what happens when that injury or illness siphons your time away with no end in sight?

Losing control over my schedule disoriented me as much as anything else in the early days of rehabbing an injury and addressing the underlying disease. I lived in eastern New Mexico. My closest specialists were in Amarillo, about a two-hour drive. My surgeon for my hips was in Albuquerque, a three-and-a-half-hour drive. I was a full-time pastor with all the responsibilities I had before my injuries. I also taught a class every semester at Eastern New Mexico University. I had an active family. None of these things took a vacation because I needed to see a doctor. I simply had to absorb the loss of time by working whenever and however I could.

A preacher's life—like many professions—has a rhythm to it. Each sermon had an allotted amount of time. I needed to get it done and be ready to preach it by Sunday. If I was also teaching a Sunday or Wednesday Bible class, time would have to be apportioned accordingly. Then there were the pastoral duties, which included visiting those who were shut-in, hospitalized individuals, and meeting with others who had spiritual needs. There were also various ministries I was leading or contributing to outside of my core duties. If all was going well, and I didn't have an unexpected funeral to officiate, I might get everything done without a high level of stress. There was no leftover time for dealing with extensive illnesses and medical appointments. What happens when chronic health conditions eat away at the thin margins of time you had? I was forced to find ways to adapt as best I could.

My wife drove to my doctors' appointments as I rode in the passenger seat, with my computer on my lap and my commentaries spilling out of my book bag onto the car floor, while I worked on that week's sermon. I've taken books into doctors' offices to read while I waited for the doctor. Even if you didn't have the long drives to medical appointments like I did, constant appointments can wreck your schedule. I have felt the drain of time even while waiting to pick up prescriptions or calling my insurance company because they denied needed medical services. I once heard another preacher say that the hardest thing about being a preacher is that Sunday comes once a week. Chronic illness made it seem like the next Sunday was here when the previous one was barely over. I had recurring dreams about suddenly realizing it was time to walk up to the pulpit, only to realize that I never had the time to prepare for my sermon. For a preacher, that is a frightening dream!

I have not yet mentioned the loss of time that comes from disease itself. Some people have to reduce their workload or quit their jobs altogether. Almost all people with chronic illness cannot maintain their previous pace for daily activities. They move more slowly and need rest more often. As I mentioned above, this could cause the opposite experience of having too much time and not enough health to do anything with it. Either way, it isn't life as we envisioned it.

Then there is the loss of time for maintaining our relationships. At home, you may find yourself withdrawn from meaningful conversation and engagement with your spouse and kids. You often will not feel like going out to dinner or sitting through sports events, or if you do these things, you will pay the price later.

Single people may experience an even more devastating cost. They suffer from a diminished capacity to bond with friends and pursue meaningful relationships, but their need for that bonding is not reduced by chronic illness. Unsympathetic friends eventually move on to others who will not decline their invitations for social outings. We will talk more about this struggle in the next chapter on the loss of relationships. For now, I am pointing out that the complicating trigger for the loss of quality relationships is a decreased capacity to invest time in activities that allow most relationships to flourish.

We lose time for hobbies as well. Hobbies are not just simple pleasures to pass the time but opportunities to expand our limitations, both physically and mentally. Hobbies provide an outlet for our God-given creativity. They arouse joy in our spirits and reveal what we value enough to make time to do off the clock, so to speak. Hobbies are often shared with others we care about, so there is a relational impact when we have to give up a hobby as well.

Before I injured my hips, I was training for a ten-kilometer race, and I invested much time in taekwondo, not just for myself, but for my sons, too. It brought me joy to be physically active in developing skills that I loved. It was a connection to my childhood and the bonding that occurred between my family and me when we were involved in martial arts together. If this was all that chronic pain robbed me of, it is still a significant blow.

My middle child, Micah, had to give up marching band and playing the drums when he began to experience symptoms similar to mine. It got to the point when he could no longer hold the drumsticks because his hands were hurting so much. Playing drums wasn't just a thing Micah did; it expressed something about who he is. When we went to local football games after he was forced to quit, the sound of the band was, and still is, always bittersweet.

What hobbies have you been forced to surrender? What did you love to do that you can no longer do? Don't think for a moment that such a loss is insignificant. The time you received back for giving up a beloved hobby is in no way an equal trade. You would rather be doing what you loved doing, and that's completely understandable. Losing the ability to do what nourishes the body and soul is a loss not easily recouped.

Later, we will talk about how some of that time can be repurposed. For now, it is important to acknowledge that your way of life has been plundered by chronic illness and pain. Resist the temptation to downplay that loss. It is huge, and God sees it.

TIME AND MORTALITY

Your understanding of who God is impacts your attitude toward time and its loss. Most religions and worldviews do not worship a god who is outside of time. The angst we all experience about time and mortality is increased or decreased significantly by how you view God.

The Greeks and Romans envisioned time as a god named Chronos. Chronos was one of the original primordial gods, who existed before the more well-known pantheon of gods, which included Zeus. Chronos is envisioned as having a role in the creation of the world itself and is often depicted as an old man with a long beard holding an hourglass or a scythe, representing the inevitability of time as the destroyer of all things. No one could threaten Chronos, as the very fabric of the universe was dependent on him, not the other way around. Chronos is threatening and brings with him the certainty of mortality.[6]

In Christian theology, time is not primary or before all things. Time answers to the one Creator of all things. The Bible says a lot about time and how we use it. I will offer a theology of time in chapter 10 that is different from how Western society views it. Here, I want to survey three passages about time that demonstrate how the biblical witness is fully aware of the human plight of the brevity of time. It is inseparable from our mortality. It is tied directly to the curse of death, ushered into our experience by our rebellion in the garden of Eden.

Psalm 90 is attributed to Moses, and verse 3 recalls the mortal curse visited upon Adam and his descendants. "You return mankind to the dust, saying, 'Return, descendants of Adam.'" The next verse is the well-known "a thousand years are like a day to you" passage in reference to the timelessness of Yahweh. The scope of a human's time on earth is minuscule in comparison. Our shortened days are a result of God's wrath against our iniquities (Ps 90:7–9).

What is important for those of us who suffer from chronic health conditions to understand is that what Moses describes is

6. Moses, "Chronos."

common to the human condition. It is not particular to those who have an ongoing physical ailment. Another way to say it is that all human beings have the same physical ailment. It's called "mortality." Some people get to control their schedules more precisely and accomplish more of the things they dream about doing, yet they are still compared to withering grass that dries up in a single day (Ps 90:5–6). The author of Ecclesiastes describes the plight of mortality similarly: "For what does a person get with all his work and all his efforts that he labors at under the sun? For all his days are filled with grief, and his occupation is sorrowful; even at night, his mind does not rest. This too is futile" (Eccl 2:22–23).

Again, this isn't the dilemma of just a few unlucky people but the harsh reality of every human being. In fact, to forget this truth is to participate in boastful evil, according to James:

> Come now, you who say, "Today or tomorrow we will travel to such and such a city and spend a year there and do business and make a profit." Yet you do not know what tomorrow will bring—what your life will be! For you are like vapor that appears for a little while, then vanishes.
>
> Instead, you should say, "If the Lord wills, we will live and do this or that." But as it is, you boast in your arrogance. All such boasting is evil. So it is sin to know the good and yet not do it. (Jas 4:13–17)

James's last line is not a diversion from his argument about time. Failing to do good because you are valuing future plans you may not even have the opportunity to fulfill is sin. Recognizing that every one of us lives on borrowed time is wisdom. Yes, it is sinful to misuse the time God has given us, but it is not a sin to lose time due to factors you can't control. The sin lies in the presumption that we control the clock.

I once met a man, a retired businessman in Japan, who had put off becoming a Christian while he was still pursuing his career. He didn't want the tension of trying to be a Christian while none of his coworkers were. Think about the good he could have done for himself and his coworkers had he not let fear seduce him into the presumptuousness that he would always have time to follow

Jesus later. Of course, I believe God's grace was still available to him when he finally made his decision, but that doesn't mean there was no real loss caused by his brazen gamble.

This is the kind of person James is talking about when he says, "So it is sin to know the good yet not do it." If we've been guilty of the same thing, maybe experiencing the time distortion that comes with chronic illness and pain has humbled us. If not, we are missing an opportunity to be delivered from a dangerous folly.

Once we have been delivered from the presumptuousness of thinking we will always have the time to do what we want, we no longer need to feel shame because of the time slippage due to our health struggles. Our mortality creates this tension with time, but lost time is not a total loss. In chapter 10, we will explore how we can redeem the time we do have.

THE "I AM" AND TIME

Chronically ill people are constantly reminded that there is something wrong with their bodies. This "wrong" is not something particular to us. We are all mortal regardless of our current health, but the chronically ill person is more in touch with that reality by necessity and through painful, constant reminders.

We are living displays of evaporating vapors of time that have been made visible to us by physical maladies, which remain invisible to those who are susceptible to forgetting their own mortality. I know the experience of chronic conditions is not what we would choose, but an advantage we do have is that the illusion we were ever in control of our lives and our time has been vaporized. We do not have to struggle to grasp what Moses, the teacher of Ecclesiastes, or James meant about the brevity of life and the preciousness of time. It is a lesson reinforced daily. But does the inevitable march of time have the final say over our destiny?

I often hear the maxim, "Time is undefeated." Indeed, time reigns supreme over mere mortals. But what the Greeks and Romans could never conceive was revealed to Moses as the "I Am" (Exod 3:14). God revealed his name to Moses as Yahweh, a name derived from the Hebrew verb "to be." God always is. Even his name repels the limitations of time.

God is never on the clock. He has always been and will always be. As John heard in Revelation, God is the "one who is, who was, and is to come" (Rev 1:4). Time does not bracket God, but all time is enclosed by his outstretched hands. That perspective puts the time we lose into its proper context. Time is not an all-encompassing god like Chronos but merely a tool in the hands of the Timeless Architect.

For us, the clock is ticking, and none of us knows when time is up. We would rather spend that precious time in places other than doctors' offices and hospitals, but God meets us in all places and at all times. If we can find peace with our current reality, then we can discover a new future that not even time and death can steal from us.

REFLECTION QUESTIONS

1. How would you describe the way chronic illness has changed your experience of time? Does it feel like time slips away, slows down, or something else entirely?
2. What enjoyable activity or hobby have you had to give up—or greatly limit—because of your chronic health conditions?
3. In what ways do you see time and mortality connected in the Bible?
4. The author writes, "Recognizing that every one of us lives on borrowed time is wisdom." What does that truth mean to you personally?
5. How does God's timelessness bring you comfort when you're faced with the limits of your own time?

Chapter Four

The Loss of Relationships

The closer someone is to the center of our lives, the more they are impacted by whatever happens to us, and vice versa. Humans are inextricably linked to one another. This is God's design, but like all things affected by the fall, that design has suffered greatly.

Adam blamed Eve immediately for his sin, and husbands and wives have lived with the possibility of estrangement to the present day. Married couples are not the only people impacted. In the best of circumstances, a harmonious relationship between family members and close friends is hard to nourish. When additional stressors are added, trouble is guaranteed.

LOSS OF RELATIONSHIPS THROUGH ATTRITION

Chronic conditions do far more than add a single stressor to relationships. We have already seen how chronic conditions impact dreams, money, and time. Living with chronic illness is like choosing several of the most stress-inducing experiences and unloading them all at once on a family and then watching them gradually increase in severity. Even the best relationships are prone to crack under that kind of pressure.

Personal injury or illness is ranked sixth on the Holmes and Rahe scale, a scale that ranks stressful life events.[1] Many other events on the scale will happen to you whether or not you are dealing with chronic pain, but chronic conditions add their own stress and potentially create new stress events. We need the people in our lives to stand by us through this overwhelming storm. It affects everyone around us, but together we can help each other stay afloat. At least, that's how it's supposed to work. If you have a supportive family and network of friends, give thanks to God. Many do not have this supportive network when facing the challenge of life-altering illness and pain. Even if you do have this support system in place, it will be strained by the loss of quality time with loved ones.

You may be familiar with Gary Chapman's *The Five Love Languages*,[2] if not the book, then at least the language and terms. In no particular order, Chapman's love languages are: quality time, physical touch, acts of service, gift giving, and words of affirmation. It does not take a great imagination to visualize how all of these essential components of giving and receiving love in a relationship are impacted by chronic illness.

Quality Time

It is hard to give the attention necessary for quality time when all you are thinking about is how badly you hurt. When my pain and fatigue levels are high, I emotionally withdraw from everyone around me. It is a way of coping with the reality of diminishing emotional resources that my illnesses are draining out of my life. I struggle to communicate with my spouse and my kids about what I'm experiencing. I can't even find the right words or the energy for words at all to explain why I am distant or uninterested in protracted conversations, not to mention any kind of physical touch.

1. Cuncic, "What Is the Holmes."
2. Chapman, *Five Love Languages*.

Physical Touch

Physical touch is about more than just sexual intimacy, but sexual intimacy between a husband and wife is a vital aspect of this love language. Sexual intimacy suffers when one or both spouses feel poorly. Almost anyone I have talked to with chronic health conditions about this issue has struggled in their sex lives to some extent. Some have seen their sex lives virtually come to an end.

Any of the stressors mentioned in this book can affect the intimacy between a husband and wife. When you factor in the multitude of medicines that many with chronic conditions require and the physical impact of the disease itself, it is no surprise that sex can feel like a relic of the past for at least one of the partners. This can lead to shame and resentment between the couple, not to mention the impact of depression and other mental health conditions on sexual intimacy.

It is not within the scope of this book to discuss these problems and potential solutions, but the struggle of lost sexual intimacy needs to be acknowledged. The stigma of shame and embarrassment, feelings of neglect, believing you are at fault, etc., only add to isolation and relational pain. If this is a struggle in your marriage, I promise you are far from alone. A 2020 study found that couples (marital status not specified) where at least one of the partners had a serious health condition for six months were 40 percent more likely to break up. Yet, the researchers did not pinpoint the lack of physical intimacy alone as the cause. Many of the additional challenges that come with chronic health problems conspire together to undermine the integrity of the relationship, "including medical costs and/or the burden of caregiving."[3] The loss of sexual intimacy often becomes just another casualty of all the other fallout from chronic illness.

Regardless of the statistics or how long you have been dealing with illness, the best path forward is honest communication with your spouse. Do not let feelings of shame and resentment contribute to the breakdown of your marriage. And do not let that shame

3. Halpert, "Chronic Disease," para. 13.

keep you from talking to your doctor or counselor, who may be able to help.

Acts of Service

What about acts of service? You survived the day at work only because you fantasized about lying on your couch all day. This was what my life was like at my lowest point in 2015 and 2016. Every minute and hour of the day was a battle not to think about the constant pain in my lower back. The intensity would build the longer I sat. When I got out of my chair, it was shocking how much it hurt to get moving again.

But if I stood for very long, all of my lower body began to hurt, so I had to sit back down. When it came time to go home for the day, the only thing that sounded good to me was lying sideways on my couch. I had young children and a wife waiting on me, but I felt like I had so little to offer. Every day was focused on survival just to do it all over again the next day. My mental health began to take an enormous hit. I felt physically and emotionally overwhelmed and then had to deal with the guilt of feeling like I was coming up short as a husband and father.

My kids were too young to help with the yard. Thankfully, a friend gave us his riding lawn mower, and our yard wasn't so big that I had to sit for very long. It was my job to do the dishes, and I could usually do that without trouble, but it was hard to think creatively about how I could serve my wife and family through acts of service besides those very basic duties.

Katie has been an exemplary spouse through all of this. Even though her love language is acts of service, she has extended me a lot of grace in dealing with my illness. However, I struggled for years to express to Katie what I was experiencing physically and mentally. My counselor encouraged me to write her a letter to say the things I was having such a challenging time articulating verbally. Writing a letter might not work for everyone, but it helped our communication about what I was experiencing and how it was affecting me. The last two love languages—gift giving and words of affirmation—are just as challenging when dealing with the complications of chronic illness.

Gift Giving

Gift giving is a difficult love language for the chronically ill because money and energy are so limited. It takes energy to be thoughtful and creative, which becomes more necessary when you cannot afford to buy the kind of gifts you used to purchase. We have already discussed how our finances are affected by chronic health conditions, but this is just another way that issue comes to bear on our relationships.

It can be particularly difficult if you have someone close to you who not only loves to receive gifts but also loves to give them lavishly. Though the giver may honestly expect nothing in return or any gift of equal value, it is hard to shake the feeling that you need to give in kind. Receiving gifts can become an embarrassing experience instead of the joyful moment the gift-giver desired to give us. It might help to realize that some people have a special gift of generosity and love to bless others without the expectation of getting anything in return other than the joy of blessing someone else. Romans 12:8 instructs such a person to "give with generosity."

If giving gifts is your love language, remember that "generosity" is not attached to a particular monetary value but to the intentions of your heart. The NET renders that same verse "if it is contributing, he must do so with sincerity." It is the trappings of our materialistic culture that have made generosity more about a price tag than the heart. Even if you can't give as much as you used to, you can have the same heart when you give. Hopefully, those close to you know that is all that ever counted anyway.

Words of Affirmation

Words of affirmation are the most available resource to the sufferer, but even then, the enthusiasm of those words may be absent when you are overwhelmed by your pain. Pain demands our attention. It's hard to focus on others, whatever your love language, when pain makes you a captive audience. It may also be hard to receive words of affirmation from others when you are struggling with the burden of pain and the often accompanying depression. Depression and anxiety can make it hard to receive and give compliments.[4] The fallout from the limitations placed on the ways we are most comfortable receiving and giving love is extensive. It is important to acknowledge that relationships suffer at the hands of chronic pain even when everyone has the best intentions—as is the case for Amy and Justin.

Amy is in one of our support groups with a condition so severe that she has to lie in a dark bedroom for months at a time. Every time her husband, Justin, comes into the room to talk to her, they both have to weigh the benefit to their relationship against the cost to her well-being. Even talking to her increases her pain. While this is an extreme scenario, people with chronic illness and pain are often faced with situations where investing in a relationship can increase their degree of suffering. I have said a lot about the impact of chronic illness on marriage, but every kind of relationship is impacted.

What about hanging out with friends? Sure, if they want to sit with you on a couch and watch television while you say next to nothing, come on over! By the way, if you have a friend who will do that just to be with you, then make sure you hang on to them.

For single people, the difficulties of chronic health conditions pose a threat to more than whether they can hang out with friends. Singleness can be a gift (1 Cor 7:7) for the purpose of devotion to the Lord, but it comes with its unique challenges when chronic illness enters the picture. Since I write from the perspective of a married man with children, I cannot speak directly to this life situation. I will let the words of Christina, who is living the single life, speak to that circumstance:

> I am single, so it is really just me providing for myself. I have to choose jobs that have decent health insurance, and you usually don't get to know that information as detailed as you'd like to make an informed decision. But

4. Whitbourne, "When Praise," para. 8.

> my illnesses at their worst left me wondering who would care for me if I got too sick to work. I couldn't move in with family as my family of origin was abusive. I regularly have had to face the reality that the church would have to step up to meet my needs if complete disability is ever the outcome.

Single or married, we need to be honest about the stress chronic illness and pain places on our relationships. If we are not, if we are still operating with the assumption that nothing is different, then we are setting ourselves up for potentially catastrophic disappointment. Not all relational loss is by well-meaning people locked into this intense struggle. Sometimes the relationship is fractured through a choice that chooses to avoid the struggle altogether.

LOSS OF RELATIONSHIPS THROUGH ABANDONMENT

The damage to relationships can lead to devastating consequences when a loved one abandons a hurting person. I want to be clear that I am making no excuses for those who have abandoned spouses, parents, children, siblings, or friends amid their suffering. I am not blaming the sufferer for alienating their loved ones just because they are sick. On the one hand, I want to help those of us with chronic illness recognize the seriousness of the challenge so that we can do what we can to nourish our important relationships. On the other hand, there is no excuse for the heartless abandonment so many people have had to face because someone decided, "I didn't sign up for this."

I commend those who suffer with their hurting loved ones, no matter the cost. I have known many husbands or wives who have lived out their "in sickness and in health" vow in loving, sacrificing, and heroic ways. It is easy to focus on those who flee the scene, but sadly, that is a circumstance we need to acknowledge for too many people—people like Jessica.

Jessica suffers from a combination of mysterious illnesses that render her life almost unlivable. Not only did her husband leave her in this state, but he turned her adult child against her.

Her parents and siblings decided that her health problems were all in her head and turned their backs on her, too. Now Jessica, only in her forties, struggles immensely to hold on to her faith in God. Can you blame her? I can't.

Another woman shared with a group on Facebook that her husband told her, "I didn't sign up for this." She didn't sign up for being abandoned by her husband. She did not want to face her trial as a single woman. Like Christina said above, when family support is lacking, we may have to "face the reality that the church would have to step up to meet [our] needs."

Can people really turn to their church family when they have no other family to turn to? Ideally, yes, but as we will see, it isn't that simple. Too often, the church casts aside those it may perceive as slowing them down, which adds to the pain of lost relationships the chronic illness sufferer has already experienced.

THE LOSS OF RELATIONSHIPS WITH GOD OR CHURCH

All of this talk about a church family presumes that people are significantly connected to a church. In Jessica's case, she had little time as a new Christian and limited church experience before her problems overtook her. For those who had been heavily engaged with their church, it is not uncommon to hear stories of neglect and abandonment from their churches once their problems made them a "liability" instead of an "asset."

"I mostly attend church online but feel totally ignored by the church I used to attend," Carrie wrote to me. As an important aside, when churches downplay the significance of offering online services, they are writing off people like Carrie even more. Watching a church service on your device at home is never going to be an adequate substitute for in-person worship and community, but it is certainly better than nothing!

After attending his first Broken and Mended support group, Jason wrote to me, "For the first time I feel like I was among people who truly had the exact same things in common with me: brethren who want to glorify the Lord but may feel lacking due to physical limitations and brethren who actually understand what it's like to truly have chronic pain—true empathy." If Jason's words are a positive response regarding his experience in a support group, let's keep in mind that it was made possible by a ministry that focuses on his situation. Do not miss those first words, "For the first time." Jason's discovery of an empathetic community came after years of being effectively cut off from his church due to his illness. If a person feels isolated from family, friends, and church, is it surprising that they would struggle in their relationship with God?

When it seems that everyone else has abandoned you, please know that God has not. There are no guarantees when it comes to the trustworthiness of fellow humans, but God is not fickle like us. He promised the Israelites, "For the Lord your God is the one who will go with you; he will not leave you or abandon you" (Deut 31:6), and the author of Hebrews permits us a more individual application when he quotes the same verse in the context of contentment:

> Be satisfied with what you have, for he himself has said, **I will never leave you or forsake you**. Therefore, we may boldly say,
>
> **The Lord is my helper;**
> **I will not be afraid.**
> **What can man do to me?** (Heb 13:5–6)[5]

The confident declaration of the Hebrews' author is founded on the character and promise of Jesus himself. "Immanuel," Jesus' prophetic name, means "God with us." Jesus told his disciples in the Great Commission, "And remember, I am with you always, to the end of the age" (Matt 28:20b). I cannot guarantee the chronic sufferer much in this painful journey, but I can guarantee what God himself promises upon his own holy name: he will not abandon you.

It may not always feel like God is with you. And yes, God can handle your feelings of disappointment and anger. The psalmist in Ps 22:1 cried out, "My God, my God, why have you forsaken me?"

5. Formatting and emphasis retained from the Holman Christian Standard Bible.

Those same words were taken up by our Lord on his cross. But do not stop with the first verse of a psalm if you want to know the deeper truth. Meditate on verse 24 of Ps 22:

> For he has not despised or abhorred
> the torment of the oppressed.
> He did not hide his face from him
> but listened when he cried to him for help.

God had not hidden his face from the psalmist, and Jesus was not ultimately abandoned by his Father. Likewise, God will not abandon you even when all the present circumstances claim the opposite. We often encounter God's presence through fellow believers who will not forsake us in our suffering.

Don't let your fear of disappointment keep you from asking God to lead you to others in your life who will stick by you no matter what. That is the main reason we formed the Broken and Mended ministry. I want people to know they are not alone. God himself assessed the state of his own image-bearer, the first man, and said, "It is not good for man to be alone" (Gen 2:18).

We will return to this theme in chapter 11. For now, I plead with you not to give up on your relationship with God. He has not given up on you. Satan desires to convince you otherwise, and he expertly uses other people to demoralize you to the point of giving up. Don't let him do it.

God has staked his reputation on the truth that he will never leave you. Believe him. Recall the parable of the persistent widow in Luke 18. Jesus expounds in verse 7, "Will not God grant justice to his elect who cry out to him day and night?" Then Jesus ends by placing the ball back in our court: "Nevertheless, when the Son of Man comes, will he find faith on earth?" (Luke 18:8). Why does Jesus ask that question? Because it is only through persistence in prayer that faith will prevail. When we are under attack from the evil one through chronic pain and abandonment, how much more do we need the reminder to keep going before our loving Father, who will never abandon us?

As we close this chapter, I invite you to set the book aside and spend time in prayer. The more abandoned you feel, the more you need this moment. Let God speak the assurance of his presence to your heart, right now. He will not delay in coming to your aid.

REFLECTION QUESTIONS

1. When you think about the five love languages (quality time, words of affirmation, gift giving, physical touch, and acts of service) which has become the hardest for you to give or receive because of your health challenges?
2. Which relationship in your life has been the most difficult to navigate on your chronic illness journey, and why?
3. What has your experience been with your church family (if you're part of one) in relation to your chronic condition—mostly positive, negative, or a mix of both?
4. Have you ever struggled to believe Jesus' promise that he would never abandon you? What has made that promise harder or easier to trust?
5. Do you have a friend or loved one who has faithfully walked beside you through your illness or pain? If so, how might you let them know what their support has meant to you?

Chapter Five

The Loss of Dignity

AN EMBARRASSING EXPERIENCE

My memory is a little fuzzy on the details, but, as much as I would like to forget it, the experience is unforgettable. I had been in the infusion room at my rheumatologist clinic a half dozen times or so. I had never had an issue, except with the intravenous steroids, which we eliminated after the first infusion of Remicade. Remicade had delivered me out of a year-long flare, and I had no intentions of changing this important therapy.

I was reclining in my infusion chair with the IV jabbed into my right arm, the medicine hanging in a clear bag from a pole with wheels in case I needed to head to the bathroom over the two-and-a-half-hour treatment. There were a half dozen patients scattered around the open room in their infusion chairs, including a young woman I had never seen before. It might have been her first time there, but for some reason, she seemed out of place in such a somber room.

The room was not particularly cool or warm, but I began to feel my body warming uncomfortably about thirty minutes into the infusion. I was reading a book on my Kindle, but soon I became concerned about the growing nausea overtaking me. The nurses checked in on you every once in a while, and I had already told mine I was fine a few minutes ago. I quickly realized there would be no time to flag her down for help and no time to make a run for the bathroom.

I rarely vomit, but there's no mistaking the inevitable feeling when it is going to happen immediately. I only had time to grab the small trash can next to my chair and let it go. I may not vomit often, but there is no going quietly into the night for me when it does happen! I am sure there are people who vomit louder than me, but I just haven't met any yet! When I finally finished, I looked up at a room full of horrified faces. The wide-eyed young woman looked like she wanted to run, and even the nurses acted like they had never seen anything like it before. Unfortunately, that was not the end of this unpleasant ordeal.

Next came waves of back pain that went far beyond my normal disease experience. When the nurses finally sprang into action, they disconnected the Remicade and started administering anti-nausea medicine and some kind of pain medicine for my back. They brought me a wet rag and a fan. I waited desperately for the nausea to pass.

The next day, I was at my emergency room with appendicitis. I thought that was what had caused the episode in the infusion room, so I optimistically returned on schedule six weeks later, and the same thing nearly happened again. This time, they got the anti-nausea medicine to me in time, but I was in horrible pain for the next three days. It was the end of Remicade therapy for me.

EMBARRASSMENT AND THE LOSS OF DIGNITY

The vomiting scene was embarrassing. I was embarrassed that I had made such a scene and had been the center of attention over something that was probably nauseating to everyone there. It was a temporary experience of the loss of dignity. And that is so often at stake with chronic illnesses and their invasive procedures.

I am an easily embarrassed person, but I don't even like people to know that I am embarrassed. Whatever happens, I want to project a "We've all been there" vibe. Try doing that right after you've just puked your guts out in front of the whole room! So, if you're the type who feels embarrassed if someone notices how long you've been in the bathroom, then you are in good company with me! The problem is that chronic illness doesn't care about your embarrassment. It delights in stripping away your dignity.

I have Crohn's disease, and one of the consequences is that I do spend a lot of time in the bathroom. I would rather you not know that, but there is no sense guarding my dignity when one of the main reasons I'm writing this book is to let you know that you are not alone. Maybe you don't have Crohn's, but if you've spent any time in hospitals at all or had invasive medical procedures, then you have experienced the loss of dignity to some degree.

My wife reminds me that this is just an expected reality for women, and, even more so, for those who give birth. So, I am acknowledging that this loss is more commonplace for women. Healthy men can maybe hide from this medical loss of dignity, but it needs to be acknowledged for all of us because it can get a lot worse than any of us wants to imagine. We've all had to slip on that hospital gown, the ones with the open back. I've even had to get help because my shoulders do not permit me to reach far enough to tie the strings in the back.

I have been whisked by waiting rooms in my hospital bed on the way to the operating room. It feels like everyone is watching, wondering, "What's going to happen to that guy?" Then, when you arrive in the cold room, full of medical staff, with machines beeping and bright lights everywhere, and the coverings have to come off, there's no pretense of dignity. The best part is knowing that you are about to be knocked out until it is over, and you wake up with your covers back in place in the recovery room.

I have known both children and adults who have lost control of their bowels and bladder due to their conditions and treatments. Being in a public place became a horror for them. Their parents, spouses, or other medical professionals, who had to clean up their mess, feel embarrassed for them, no matter how great their empathy and love are. However, experiencing the loss of dignity is not just about embarrassing accidents or being forced to wear revealing clothing at the hospital. Losing the ability to fulfill the basic functions of the roles we have in life lasts much longer and reaches far deeper.

God has given me many opportunities to listen to the stories of men who have been devastated by an illness or health condition that sent their world spinning out of control. All of a sudden, they couldn't be the husband or father they thought they should be. This induces shame even if they have the most supportive wife. Sometimes, the more supporting and sacrificial the wife is, the more the husband may feel shame for not being able to do his part in the marriage and home. A man named Rick, whom I interviewed for this book, experienced this inner shame in his relationship with his wife.

Rick, now in his mid-sixties, had a life-altering back injury caused by a surgery in his mid-fifties in 2016. Rick was a successful executive for Toyota with a job that required a lot of travel. Soon, his degenerative back condition made that impossible. The first blow was seeing his salary cut by 50 percent. Rick held out for a couple of years after his injury, hoping to salvage his career, even though it had become nearly impossible for him to work. "I couldn't emotionally let go of the job," he told me, but by 2018, his disability claimed his career. Rick experienced this as a shameful defeat. "I was walking out with my tail between my legs," he told me. His identity was tied up in his career. Rick felt like he was "losing a part of myself."

As I have already pointed out several times in this book, the losses we experience due to life-altering chronic pain rarely stop with just imploding one area of our lives. Rick recalled his state of mind in 2018 and the following years as having "no life, no ability to socialize, and being robbed of interests." This was compounded by how quickly his coworkers, who had known him for years, forgot him and his suffering.

Rick and his wife had bought land in Prescott, Arizona, where they could live an active life when he retired. They had to give up on that dream and sell their land. This is a loss he is still mourning. By 2021, the disappointment, the grief, the shame, and the pain all led to Rick praying "for God to take me." Rick's story illustrates nearly all the losses we have detailed to this point in the book, but what stood out to me is how he experienced the loss of his career and mobility with a deep sense of shame. Having a supportive wife did not mitigate that loss of dignity.

Today, it may be just as common for women's identities to be tied to their careers in our society, but around the world, women often have their own circumstances that contribute to shame. Culture often dictates expectations for the different roles we fill. Wives and mothers, like Eunice, experience the same shame when they cannot fulfill the roles they want to fill or the cultural expectations of their society.

I met Eunice in Kenya, who lamented her inability to carry water on her head or keep up with the children, the cooking, and the tasks that nearly every other woman in her community performed. When she could not carry out those responsibilities, she not only experienced internal shame but was shamed by her community who decided she must be less of a woman because she couldn't do the same as the other women. The loss of dignity and the experience of guilt and shame may differ from culture to culture, but this loss is often devastating to someone already living with constant physical pain.

Some have only momentary moments of losing their dignity or experiencing embarrassment, while others have ongoing battles with a deep sense of shame internally, like Rick, or societal shame from failing to meet cultural expectations, like Eunice. Whatever the particular experience, almost all who have ongoing chronic illnesses experience this degradation in some way, and that's without anyone trying to make it worse with insensitivity or cruelty. We feel shame acutely in our society and experience social shame for not carrying out cultural expectations. Honor and shame had an even greater hold on the societies addressed in the Bible.

SHAME IN THE BIBLE

The Bible was written to cultures steeped in honor/shame paradigms. For these people, it was serious to lose their dignity. Not every embarrassment rises to the level of shame, but they closely overlapped in ancient Near Eastern cultures. The Hebrew word translated "be ashamed" by the Christian Standard Bible is *bosh.* It is particularly present in the book of Jeremiah. It does not only denote an inner experience or shame but a real loss of dignity and position in their society.[1]

The first time *bosh* is used is Gen 2:25, where we are told that "Both the man and his wife were naked, yet felt no shame [*bosh*]." Unfortunately, this positive statement also foreshadows the arrival of shame in the very next chapter, riding in on the coattails of sin and rebellion. That shame was tied to Adam and Eve's sexuality—specifically, their nakedness. Prior to their downfall, they knew no shame, but now they covered up from each other and hid from God (Gen 3:1–13). Shame was here to stay for a very long time and remains with us to this day.

That story is not in the Bible just to tell us what happened to Adam and Eve. It is there so we can understand the origins of our own shame. When God made the body, he assessed it as he did everything else in creation: it was good. God did not intend for his image bearers to be ashamed of their bodies or their needs. Sin changed all that, and our dignity has been under assault ever since.

Now we shame each other. We mock and ridicule others, even in childhood, to bolster our standing with our peers at the expense of those we dishonor. Because of this, we all develop abject insecurities, which lead us to hide in the bushes, so to speak. We hide from those insecurities, or we perpetuate the cycle by attacking others we deem weaker than ourselves.

We grow out of some of these behaviors, most of the time, but we carry those deep insecurities with us through life. We feel shame for things that are not our fault, and chronic illness exacerbates our feelings of guilt in nearly every area of our lives. We can't play with our kids the way we used to: shame. Our family is now on the brink of financial ruin: guilt. I need help cleaning up because I didn't make it to the bathroom in time: embarrassment. These indignities compound and can lead to feelings of worthlessness.

1. *Christian Study Bible*, 1155.

WHEN GOD CHOSE SHAME

We will revisit these issues in chapter 12, but for now, I remind you that God has not left us alone in our shame. The incarnation is not just that Jesus became human, which is miraculous and mysterious enough. Jesus went further. He endured temptation, though he did not sin (Heb 4:15). This fact is not only about Jesus passing a test that every other human has failed, but he endured temptation so he could "empathize with our weaknesses" (Heb 4:15 NIV).

Jesus' embrace of the human experience goes even further. To be crucified was to be shamed in the most extreme manner in the first-century Roman Empire. The victim was displayed naked publicly while still living. There was no lower point for a person to descend than to a Roman cross. When Paul wrote about it to the Philippians, he describes Christ's descent from the form of God to being found in the form of a slave. Paul tells his readers he became obedient to death, "even death on a cross!" (Phil 2:8 NET). Or to use the author of Hebrews' explicit language of shame: "For the joy that lay before him, he endured the cross, despising the shame, and sat down at the right hand of the throne of God" (Heb 12:2).

We suffer through the loss of dignity because we have no choice. We experience shame because it is an existential reality in a world of sin. Jesus did not have to endure any loss of dignity, but he chose to do so for us in obedience to his Father. He chose the lowest point of human dignity available and took our shame upon himself at the cross. We may not experience the depths of shame that Jesus did while on the cross, but we still feel our loss of dignity acutely.

Perhaps we guard our dignity too fiercely, considering that the one we follow gave his up willingly. I do not mean to diminish the feelings of embarrassment and shame we experience in situations caused by our chronic health conditions, which many of our healthy contemporaries may never have to discover, but I am calling for perspective. The loss is real, but our felt experiences are not the total picture of reality. When we are ashamed, we often do so with exaggerated emotions because of how deeply personal we all feel shame.

Jesus' embrace of shame that did not belong to him means he purposely identified with us when he did not have to. It means he embraced shame because he knew it was not the end of the story. It is not the end of our story either. Our shame does not receive the last word. A shameless future beckons.

REFLECTION QUESTIONS

1. When have you felt embarrassment related to your medical condition? Is it something you find easy or difficult to talk about?
2. If you've ever felt shame over no longer being able to fulfill certain roles or responsibilities, what do you think is at the root of that feeling?
3. How do you see sin and shame connected in the Bible?
4. What does it mean to you that God chose to enter our shame through Jesus and the cross?
5. Is there any shame you're still holding on to that God may be inviting you to release today?

Chapter Six

The Loss of Mental Health

WHEN DEPRESSION BECOMES THE BACKGROUND

Perhaps it was a coincidence, but perhaps not. As I prepared to write this chapter, I was met with a two-week bout of deepening depression. A cloud followed me around in everything I did. It was hard to focus on writing a sermon. It was hard to connect with my family, let alone with those to whom I was supposed to minister. Everything was a battle, and nearly every incident made the situation worse. Then, suddenly, it lifted exactly two weeks after it started.

People who do not understand depression think it is just a bad mood that can be overcome with a better outlook or a better spiritual attitude. But depression and other mental health disorders are as palpable as twisting your ankle. You remember exactly when you did it. Imagine someone telling you that your sprained ankle wouldn't hurt if you just considered a Bible verse about remaining thankful in all circumstances (1 Thess 5:18)! It is just as absurd to suggest such a tactic will eliminate or reduce depression. Still, biases have conditioned many to categorize it as something for which the sufferer shares the blame.

Recently, I underwent testing for ADHD. In my case, my symptoms were mild (though ever-present), but I still wanted it medically confirmed. However, ADHD wasn't all that I was being tested for. When the psychiatrist came into the room to discuss my results, I was surprised to learn that I tested high for depression with anxious distress.

Previously, I had identified incidents like the two-week trial I mentioned at the start of this chapter as my true depressive episodes. What I have learned now about myself is that depression is always in the background. It became a new normal, but when certain stressors were added—I had just recently changed careers—I began to experience depression and, apparently, anxiety in a more acute state. I was already taking medicine that helps with depression, but without these aids, I cannot be sure how bad my mental health might become.

For many, depression becomes a constant presence for those already suffering from debilitating diseases. There are many causes, some internal and some circumstantial, but it is not something you choose, and it doesn't disappear just because you aren't "doing depression" anymore. I heard this phrase on a television interview after a well-known person passed away.[1] The one paying tribute said, "She didn't do depression." Such comments demonstrate a lack of understanding of how depression works and are dismissive of those who are living with depression, as if they could also say, "I'm just not going to do depression anymore." When we speak about depression this way, we are impacting real people—often people of deep faith.

WHEN THE COST IS HUMAN LIFE

My great-uncle Billy was a man of great faith. I loved talking to Billy at family gatherings. Unlike the majority of my relatives (and unlike most people in general), he was very comfortable having deep discussions about faith. Because I had learned to associate suicide with weak faith or lack of faith, you can imagine how shocked I was to learn that one of the most spiritual people in my family had walked into the woods and shot himself.

1. Totenberg, "'She Really Didn't.'"

Suicide always leaves a lot of questions, and people who are close enough to a situation to know some of the details usually don't reveal much. The only answer I ever got when I asked why Billy had taken his own life was that he had chronic headaches. That the pain was too much to bear was all anyone could offer in explanation.

Maybe it was the pain, but now I know a little more about depression and suicide. If I had to guess, Billy was not only dealing with the severity of the pain but also mental illness brought about by chronic pain. I know it is hard for those of us who grew up associating such tragedies with spiritual failure, but Billy's actions at the end of his life were not connected with a lack of faith. If anything, his faith had helped him hold on for as long as he did.

That does not mean that Billy's suicide or anyone's suicide was inevitable. The answer is not blaming Billy or those who, theoretically, were close enough to prevent it. We simply want to tip the scales back in our favor as much as possible. How can we reduce tragic outcomes involving mental health and chronic conditions? And is there anything we can do to help those of us living with depression and/or anxiety daily, just like our other health conditions? The answer begins by understanding and acknowledging the problem without judging the sufferer.

My friend, Jeremy Harrison, wrote a brief and helpful book called *Rethinking Depression*. In the chapter called "Reframing Depression," he wrote, "People battling depression feel enough guilt and shame without being made to feel that their condition is merely a matter of simply choosing to feel better."[2] That same chapter ends with a word of hope, once we have properly *reframed depression*: "The deepest shadows of the dawn signify that the sunrise is coming. . . . Keep talking about it. Keep praying. Keep seeking. Keep living."[3]

2. Harrison, *Rethinking Depression*, 32.

3. Harrison, *Rethinking Depression*, 32.

CHRONIC PAIN AND MENTAL HEALTH: THE RESEARCH

I am a biblically educated and theologically trained pastor with a heart for people struggling with chronic illness and pain, but I am not a counselor, and I do not have any special training in psychological studies. I can speak from my experience, but that can only take us so far. However, the research backs up what others and I are experiencing; people with chronic pain and illness are fighting to overcome mental health conditions more often than not. Medical imaging indicates that pain and mental health share "biological mechanisms," which means that as pain increases, not only do we become more susceptible to depression, but our depression can also make us more sensitive to pain.[4] A downward spiral begins as pain and depression feed off each other.

Though the number of people suffering from depression and anxiety is high in the general population, chronic pain increases the risk exponentially. Mental Health America (MHA), a leading nonprofit in the field, stated, "Research shows that those with chronic pain are four times more likely to have depression or anxiety than those who are pain-free."[5] Let's not rush past that appalling number; you, the chronic pain sufferer, are four times more likely to experience depression or anxiety than pain-free people.

Why? It goes back to what this book has claimed up to this point. The losses due to chronic pain are far more than just the pain, but even when focusing on just the physical manifestations of chronic disease, the toll can feel insurmountable. MHA also points out that it is "also common for people with chronic pain to have sleep disturbances, fatigue, trouble concentrating, decreased appetite, and mood changes. These negative changes in your lifestyle can increase your pain and dampen your overall mood; the frustration of dealing with this can result in depression and anxiety."[6]

4. American Psychiatric Association, "Chronic Pain," para. 1.
5. Mental Health America, "Chronic Pain," para. 2.
6. Mental Health America, "Chronic Pain," para. 5.

If a sufferer is unable to reach out for help, or efforts to treat their health are ineffective, "mental defeat" looms as a dangerous threat. Mental defeat involves not only feeling overwhelmed to the point of hopelessness but also believing that chronic illness and pain are threatening to eradicate one's identity.[7] In other words, mental defeat is an existential crisis.

Mental defeat can be a precursor to suicide, and it is more strongly associated with chronic pain itself than other mental health conditions without chronic pain as a factor.[8] Due to this confluence of dangerous factors, all brought into play by chronic health conditions, suicidal ideation ranges from 18 percent to 50 percent in patients with chronic pain.[9] The Cleveland Clinic defines suicidal ideation as "when you think about, consider, or feel preoccupied with the idea of suicide and death."[10] These thoughts can range in intensity and severity. Most people do not act on these thoughts, but they are certainly an indication of someone needing help. The combination of chronic pain and mental health conditions is a deadly threat we cannot ignore. Unfortunately, that is too often what the church does.

THE CULPABILITY OF THE CHURCH

The two biggest responses I have ever received after a sermon came after I preached about chronic illness/pain and depression/mental health, respectively. In both cases, the people who talked to me afterward told me they had never heard their struggles acknowledged in church before. I had certainly brought them up at different points in my preaching career but never to the degree that I did when I preached those two sermons. Acknowledging physical and mental health is apparently out of place at church. Why?

Our anemic theology of the body is a primary contributor to this problem. This is surprising given that Christianity is grounded

7. Themelis et al., "Mental Defeat," 2080.
8. Themelis et al., "Mental Defeat," 2080.
9. Themelis et al., "Mental Defeat," 2080.
10. Cleveland Clinic, "Suicidal Ideation," para. 1.

in the hope of bodily resurrection. C. S. Lewis once wrote, "Christianity is almost the only one of the great religions which thoroughly approves of the body—which believes that matter is good, that God himself once took on a human body, that some kind of body is going to be given to us even in heaven and is going to be an essential part of our happiness."[11] Yet, somehow, Platonic influences have misled the church, especially the Evangelical Church, into over-spiritualizing almost everything. And when things get over-spiritualized, everything is treated as a spiritual problem, including chronic pain and illness, but especially mental health struggles.

I attended a funeral after a tragedy in which multiple family members were killed. The officiating pastor dramatically and emotionally described our bodies as nothing but vehicles you use until they wear out and are discarded like an old car. This was intended to comfort the grieving family, who lost their loved ones in a fire. If this is the view of the body, then it is no wonder suffering in the body gets little acknowledgment beyond the bulletin's prayer requests.

I'm afraid the church has often been even less helpful on the mental health front. John Piper is a well-respected pastor and theologian who has had a tremendous positive spiritual influence on many people. So, I share the following example with all due respect and only as an example of a larger pattern affecting so much of the church. Piper's view below is probably more nuanced than one interview can represent, and, of course, his view may have changed since that interview—it was given in 2007. However, we must choose our words carefully any time we are talking about mental health, and I believe Piper could have been more careful on this occasion.

Piper responded to a question about Charles Spurgeon's well-known struggle with depression. He acknowledged there was a physical dimension to Spurgeon's depression, including his battle with gout. However, the conversation shifted to addressing depression as needing to "clear the clouds" to see the object of our faith

11. Lewis, *Mere Christianity*, 91.

better (Jesus). Piper stated, "All discouragement and depression is related to the obscuring of our hope, and we need to get those clouds out of the way and fight like crazy to see clearly how precious Christ is."[12]

However, this well-intentioned theological language can dangerously miss its mark for those who need pointing toward resources that can help holistically. In Piper's remarks, there was no mention of the potential need for counseling, let alone medicine in dealing with depression. It was framed primarily as a spiritual problem that, though having physical triggers, could only be solved spiritually. Framing depression primarily as a problem of spiritual perception places the burden back on the sufferer—at precisely the moment when depression has robbed them of their capacity to "fight like crazy."

I've heard this same framing echoed by pastors, counselors, and well-meaning Christians across denominations and traditions. This approach reflects an inadequate understanding of mental health in general and depression specifically. It becomes an obstacle that keeps people from getting the potentially lifesaving help they need. Anyone who has struggled with significant depression knows how it differs from spiritual discouragement. Depression can rob a person of the will to "fight like crazy," leaving what little energy remains focused on finding relief through resources such as counseling and medication. Depression and other mental health issues are often addressed in harmful ways, but the truth is they are hardly addressed at all.

Preachers "once a year, rarely, or never" address mental health in sermons or other large group messages.[13] Ed Stetzer, who specializes in providing resources for both churches and church leaders in a myriad of ways, discusses the issue of mental health and stigma in a more balanced way. He summarizes the issue well:

> The more Christians struggle with how to deal with mental illness, the more we fail to create a safe and healthy environment in which to discuss and deal with

12. Piper, "Can Christians Be Depressed?"

13. Stetzer, "Christian Struggle."

> these issues. As a result, many of our Christian churches, homes, and institutions promulgate an aura of mistrust, guilt, and shame.[14]

Stetzer is not giving up hope that the church can change, as his next words illustrate: "As more of us are coming forward with our own stories of struggle and pain, I'm encouraged that it's okay to talk about these things. We have to defeat the shame because the reality is that many Christians struggle with mental illness."[15]

This is the church at its best—a community that defeats shame rather than perpetuating it. I am aware and sensitive to the fact that what I have written above may come across harshly. Most of my examples in this book of what churches have done or not done are unflattering ones. That's chiefly because I am emphasizing a particular problem, but I want to stress that I have a very high view of the church, which is called the body of Christ (1 Cor 12:12–26), the spiritual temple (Eph 2:21), and the bride of the Lamb (Rev 19:9; 21:2) in various New Testament texts.

When the church lives up to its identity, it's a beautiful thing. I just read a story yesterday about a church rallying behind a young woman whose eye was severely injured on a mission trip. They prayed relentlessly for her and saw to all her needs. She did not make a full recovery, but her eye and most of her vision were saved. No doubt the loving care of her church played a huge role in her recovery.[16]

But it is also true that I have heard too many stories from chronically ill and mentally ill church members who feel forgotten by their church. So, we have to talk about it. I was in pastoral church ministry for over twenty years, and I failed many times to be the caring minister I should have been, especially before I experienced chronic pain myself. So, I have been part of the problem as a part of God's church. However, when the church "rejoice[s] with those who rejoice and mourn[s] with those who mourn" (Rom 12:15), it is a powerful witness to the world of a transformative gospel. The

14. Stetzer, "Christian Struggle," para. 9.

15. Stetzer, "Christian Struggle," para. 10.

16. Furman, *Being There*, 123.

late biblical scholar Walter Brueggemann named these the three prophetic tasks of the church, as quoted in Zahnd: "tell the truth in a society that lives in an illusion, grieve in a society that practices denial, and express hope in a society that lives in despair."[17]

I believe the chronically ill members of the church can help to call the church back to these tasks. The key is getting the church to understand why it needs its chronically ill members.

THE COMPOUNDING TOLL OF THE BATTLE

The ongoing battle with pain and illness takes an incalculable toll on the sufferer. Like a compounding interest rate, you end up paying many times the cost of the pain itself. It is difficult to escape the loss of ideal mental health in this context. Matters can escalate dangerously as depression and anxiety further isolate the individual from those who might be able to help.

The church in North America has not excelled in acknowledging either chronic illness or mental health issues. When it has acknowledged these issues, the church has too often further isolated the sufferer by framing such struggles, especially those involving depression and anxiety, as a symptom of a defective faith.

There are signs that this stigmatization in the church is changing as more people become educated about the true nature of mental illnesses. As more pastors and church leaders courageously share their stories of struggle, the Christians in the pew, or watching from home, start to realize they are not alone. This is an urgent need for culture change. Lives hang in the balance.

I will return to the subject of mental health and chronic physical conditions in chapter 13, but don't wait to get help. Talk to a compassionate friend or family member. If you have a pastor or minister you can trust, reach out to them. Talk to your doctor and seek out counseling. Help is available to give you as many advantages as possible in this all-too-important struggle.

Finally, if you are contemplating suicide, don't wait to get help. Tell those closest to you what is going on. In the United

17. Zahnd, *Wood*, 12–13.

States, you can call 988, the suicide and crisis hotline. Your life is worth fighting for. Don't give up. You are not alone!

REFLECTION QUESTIONS

1. How has your mental or emotional health been affected by your chronic illness?
2. How have you understood the connection between mental health challenges like depression or anxiety and your faith?
3. Why do you think separating physical problems from mental or emotional ones can lead to misunderstanding or stigma about mental health?
4. What has your experience been like in your church community when it comes to mental health—positive, negative, or somewhere in between?
5. What is one step you could take today to make sure you're receiving the support you need for your mental and emotional well-being?

Interlude

A Funeral for What You Lost

There are moments you always recall in vivid detail. My wife and I were having dinner at the house of another couple. I kept getting missed calls from a Dallas number, and, as it almost always is, I thought it was spam, but it was strange that it was from the same number. Without really thinking about it, I decided to check my email on my phone. I saw the email was from my best friend's sister. When I connected that message to the missed calls, I knew it was nothing good.

I returned the call, standing in the backyard of our good friends and fellow church members, and Chris's sister answered. I heard the brokenness in her voice, but her message was to the point: "David, Chris was in a motorcycle accident, and he didn't make it."

I had known Chris for over twenty years. We had served in campus ministry together, served on mission trips overseas together, and we were in each other's weddings. Chris had gone through two divorces, and I was his confidant through both of them. Chris supported me through my chronic illness struggles, and he created the original logo for Broken and Mended. Over several years, we had spoken to each other on the phone nearly every week. Just a few months before the accident, those calls had ceased when Chris's new job made them difficult to schedule.

How do you process "he didn't make it" when one of the most important people in your life is just gone? I had no clue. Chris and I lived a bit under three hundred miles apart when he died. He was cremated, and so the service was planned for a couple of weeks after the accident. During those two weeks, I felt so disconnected from everyone in his family and our mutual friends. Every day, I had to convince myself that the news was real. I was stuck in limbo.

I officiated at his memorial service. When I walked into the room and saw his family for the first time since the accident, and his children crying at a table, it became very real. I was unable to move forward with my life until we had that funeral. That was over six years ago, and I still think about Chris all the time, but I try to live my life in a way that honors our friendship and our common faith in the hope of being reunited one day.

I am going to propose to you something that may be uncomfortable. In fact, it may be what you have been avoiding all along. You need a funeral for your former life. It is the only way you may be able to move forward and discover the blessings God still has in store for you. You don't want to be stuck in limbo between the life you wanted and the life that's still possible.

Coauthor of *Hope When It Hurts,* Sarah Walton, shares about the losses and grief she and her husband experienced over their son's long-term neurological disorder on a post from her website called "Frozen in Grief." She describes a concept she learned from Dr. Pauline Boss called "ambiguous loss." Ambiguous loss refers to an ongoing loss that doesn't have a singular moment to define it, like the loss of my friend. Chronic illness fits perfectly into that concept because you experience the loss over and over again. When living with ambiguous loss, you need a process to grieve and acknowledge it before you can move forward. Here's how Sarah described the stakes for her and her family:

> If I continue to live in that state grumbling and discontentment, choosing to fixate on what's been lost rather than accepting what God has allowed, my peace and joy are the first to go. I know all too well the temptation to distract myself from my reality or to focus on how things

> used to be (or how I expected them to be). But if we dwell on the life we desire, rather than the life God has chosen for us, then we miss out on seeing and experiencing the life-changing presence, grace, and blessings that he has for us right where we are.[1]

Sarah isn't exactly recommending a funeral for our past life, but she is definitely advising us to recognize what is in the past so that we can move forward into God's blessings in the present. That's the message I am trying to convey also.

This is what I mean by saying you may need a funeral for your past life. When I spoke to one of our support groups about this concept, one man raised a dilemma. His health did not move steadily in a degenerative direction. He had periods when he would feel better, and some of his old life could resume. So, how can you have a funeral for your past life when your old life keeps getting out of the grave?

No metaphor is perfect. I don't want to oversimplify the complexities of our individual circumstances. Yet, it is still true that there was a part of his old life that he could not recover because he knew that his improved health had an expiration date, even if he didn't know exactly when it was. His health was now caught up in a cycle, which was, in fact, his new reality.

Even if your illness fluctuates, there is likely a version of your life that is gone forever. If a full funeral feels premature, perhaps you can mourn the specific losses you know are permanent. But when you know your former life or the life you dreamed about is not coming back, then it is time to have that funeral.

I don't mean to literally have a funeral service. I recommend writing a letter saying goodbye to the life that was or the life you wanted to have. If it seems like a morbid exercise, understand that it is a means to an end. The entire second half of this book will explore the blessings we can gain in our chronic illness journey. But that will mean little to you if you are still holding on to what can no longer be.

1. Walton, "Frozen in Grief," para. 6.

One reservation could be that you are afraid of what it implies about God if he has a purpose for you through your suffering. Maybe you feel God didn't give you his best, and you are afraid to settle for second-best. Or maybe you are afraid that you are giving up hope for healing or remission. As I mentioned in the preface, we are all on different parts of our chronic illness journey. For myself, I do not have any reason to believe healing is coming at this time. That does not mean that I don't sometimes feel better, and it doesn't mean there won't be another season when I actively seek God's healing, but the life I knew before all this happened is not coming back, even if some aspects could be recovered.

Wherever you are in this struggle, it is always a matter of trust. Will you trust God to walk with you through your pain and to reveal hidden blessings along the way? Someone once told me that when going through a horrible loss, she figured she had to go through it with or without God, and she would rather go through it with him than without him.

You decide. Do you want to continue to live between what is no longer possible and what is still possible? Or do you want to discover purpose even amid a journey you did not choose? If you choose the latter, you will find God never intends to give his children second-best. It's just that his best is not what is most desirable in the eyes of our world. Recall the words of Jesus, "Peace I leave with you. My peace I give to you. I do not give to you as the world gives. Don't let your heart be troubled or fearful" (John 14:27). If you decide to walk this journey, what should such a letter look like? It will be different for every person, but I will share my letter to my former life with the hope that it will help guide your way.

IN MEMORIAM

To My Life Before Chronic Pain and Illness:

I liked our life. In fact, in many ways, I loved it. I was so excited to explore the possibilities in my healthy body. Before my life was irrevocably changed, I was the fittest I had ever been as an adult. I don't know if I would have remained a runner, but I was absolutely on board for a life of taekwondo. I believed martial arts not only connected my childhood with my present life as a father but would be central to my ministry career. Taekwondo was to become the connecting point to a future church planting effort I had dreamed about for a long time.

Our financial situation wasn't perfect, but there was a way out of debt, and we were making progress. The light at the end of that tunnel became a bone-jarring dead end. I hope I may be out of debt one day, but it will take decades longer than I expected.

My life with my wife and my kids was the most beautiful part of it. We had our whole future ahead of us. Anything seemed possible for us, but it was the simple things I missed out on: playing catch with my boys, continuing to achieve new successes together in taekwondo, taking my daughter to whatever activities she wanted to be involved in, dates with my wife, and vacations with my family, when never a thought of pain entered my mind.

I miss my life with few mental health struggles. What was my life like before pain entered nearly every moment of my life? How do I keep depression in check? How can I stay optimistic for the future when it looks nothing like I imagined?

But my life did not end when I lost you, the life I wanted, to chronic illness and pain. I must move on with a different life than I had and surrender the one I wanted. I honor you as the life that might have been, but I cannot hold on to you any longer. God has given me a different path to walk, and saying goodbye to you is the only way I can walk it. I won't forget you, but I must see things differently now.

One day in the resurrected life, my body will be healed and made immortal, my debts completely erased, and my relationships will know nothing but pure joy, but until that day, I do not want to miss out any longer on a single blessing God wants to give me. So, goodbye for now; I know what I lost. I need to discover what I can gain.

With warm regards,
David Heflin

Part Two

Embracing What Is Gained

Chapter Seven

The Gain of Knowing God for Who He Is

It may sound counterintuitive to talk about what you gain through your chronic illness journey. That is why I placed so much emphasis on the importance of acknowledging what we have lost. By talking about what is gained in our relationship with God, others, and our purpose for living, I do not downplay the grief and suffering your chronic condition has sown in your life.

However, if we want to enjoy the life that remains for us, we must move forward in faith and hope that God is still at work in our lives. Our suffering is fertile ground for God to do even more amazing work in our lives than possible in times of prosperity. I have known many who were adversely affected by their illness or injury in a life-altering way who later said they wouldn't go back and change what happened to them. How can they arrive at such a perspective? Because they have witnessed the power of God at work in their weakness, and it has forever changed them.

BILLIE'S STORY

I met Billie Courtright in a Weight Watchers meeting in the fall of 2007 when I was a preacher in Palm Springs, California. I was there for obvious reasons. Billie was there because he weighed over four hundred pounds.

Our meeting was a direct answer to prayer. It was my first night to attend, and I asked God if there was anyone he specifically wanted me to meet to make it happen. Billie later told me that when I walked into the room, he sensed a spiritual aura about me. No one has ever told me that before or since! God was at work in an unusual way!

The only open seat was next to Billie. I asked if I could sit there, and he welcomed me right away. We introduced ourselves, and a friendship was born. I'd love to tell you the whole story of how Billie was eventually converted to Christ and was faithful until his death several years later, but for our purposes, I just want to focus on one critical part of his story.

Billie was a professional singer and pianist. He enjoyed a successful career for decades until he suffered from a chronic disease, which robbed him of his singing voice. When I knew Billie, his voice was a raspy whisper. Because he always had cash coming in, he had not put away money during the peak of his career. He owed all kinds of money in property taxes and high-interest loans.

No one in Billie's situation chooses a disease that robs them of their livelihood. Performing for audiences had been Billie's identity. But Billie later told me, even while still suffering from the consequences of his losses, that he never would have sought God had he not lost his voice. By the time I met Billie, his identity had been stripped away, and he was looking for something or someone to fill the void.

I did not know any of this the night I had offered my prayer and met Billie. I am convinced our meeting was divinely arranged, and a life-altering chronic illness prepared the way. Billie also faithfully walked with me through the early stages of my chronic illness. When I see him again, we will both be made new and whole.

Billie's suffering prepared his way into God's kingdom, but many people come to faith during periods of relative prosperity. A serious problem emerges if this prosperity is married to a theology that disparages suffering and creates expectations for a state of uninterrupted health and wealth. When the reality doesn't match up with people's misplaced expectations, they find no place in their faith community for a theology of suffering that can make sense of their experiences. The theology that promised prosperity turned out to be bankrupt. Chronic illness exposes prosperity theology for what it is—a false view of God and the gospel of Jesus Christ—and helps us to discover what it means to know God for who he truly is.

THE BANKRUPTCY OF THE PROSPERITY GOSPEL

I once witnessed a pastor declare on Facebook in a now-deleted post that if you believe it is God's will for you to live with a disease but go to the doctor, then you are a liar. After all, why go to a doctor if you don't want to get better? And if you want to get better, then you must not accept your illness as God's will. This pastor, not surprisingly, comes from a faith tradition that is often caught up in the prosperity gospel.

There are logical problems with just about everything the pastor said in his clever syllogism, but the greatest error is the assumption that the only reason someone would go to a doctor is to be cured of their disease. He lacks the imagination to see the possibility that we might go to a doctor to manage our symptoms as best we can and to slow disease progression. We also use what can be accomplished medically on our behalf as a way of discerning God's will. If God decided to heal me through medical means, then I would understand that his will no longer requires me to carry the burden of disease.

In chapter 1, I shared Bethany's story, whose career as a missionary and then as an organ transplant coordinator ended because of her chronic illness. Both of these callings brought purpose into her life—purpose that was suddenly snatched away. There was heartbreak and disappointment with God. Bethany had much to lament.

However, through those same disappointments came a new opportunity for a meaningful career. She now works on helping patients get insurance authorization for organ transplants and coordinates their care when they are ready for discharge. It was less demanding than being on call all the time as a transplant coordinator, which led to better health and more time with her family.

Bethany has three children, but the third child was in serious jeopardy before she was even born. This is what Bethany said in her interview on *In The Seams* about how her health condition may have saved her child's life during birth:

> There were some complications of the pregnancy, very rare ones that had never even happened in the history of that medical facility. But because my tissues are looser, my womb is looser. Because I am stretchier, they were able to save her life. And she's here today because of how I am, because of how I was knit together in my mother's womb.
>
> I don't know what the Lord has for her, but I know he's got some sort of purpose because she would not be here if it weren't for the way that he made me. And so, I just like to share that story to encourage everyone that the Lord does have his hand on your life. He is guiding you, though it feels like you lose a lot. There's so much more that you're gaining through the process and that you will continue to gain.[1]

Bethany's story is a great illustration that purpose does not die when dreams do. We may not understand the purpose of our suffering in the moment, but it does not mean it isn't there. When pastors and other Christian teachers lack the imagination to believe that anything can have purpose except for miraculous healings, the power of incredible stories like Bethany's is missed. Bethany and many others have learned that not only does God not quit on them when they suffer, but he continues to work his purpose into our lives.

Unfortunately, the prosperity gospel problem is not confined to just one pastor with faulty logic like the one I mentioned above. I encounter people all the time who are told by other Christians that it is God's will to heal them in the here and now. The idea that it could be God's will to suffer faithfully with our chronic conditions

1. Heflin, "Chronic Illness."

never occurs to them. They are the victims of bad theology, and they often afflict that bad theology on people who are suffering. This is what the prosperity gospel unleashes.

The prosperity gospel, sometimes called "the health and wealth gospel," is represented by statements like this, as summarized and critiqued by Randy Alcorn: "Biblical prosperity is the ability to be in control of every circumstance and situation that occurs in life. No matter what happens, whether financial, social, physical, marital, spiritual, or emotional, this type of prosperity enables you to maintain control in every situation."[2] Statements like this one also represent the prosperity gospel: "Poverty is so unnecessary. Loss is so painful. . . . I hate pain. Your pain can stop. I want you completely healed. That's why I wrote this book."[3]

Some prosperity gospel preachers teach healing as an accomplished fact. Christ has already healed us when he died on the cross. If we don't experience healing, then it might be because we are approaching God to ask for something that he has already given instead of just claiming it. Prosperity gospel preacher and author Andy Wommack puts it this way:

> Healing has already been provided. Financial prosperity has already been provided. Joy and peace and everything that you will ever need emotionally have already been provided. If you're having a down day, if things aren't going right, if you don't feel good, you don't need to embrace discouragement, despair, and hopelessness.[4]

It is not difficult to imagine how this theology creates feelings of shame and despair amongst those who do not experience healing. Those holding to such convictions can't back down. It is obvious to them that it can only be God's will to heal you, so the problem must reside somewhere in you, the chronically ill believer. They insist your faith is lacking. You'll either have to agree with them or believe the problem is with God.

2. Alcorn, "Prosperity Theology," para. 19.
3. Alcorn, "Prosperity Theology," para. 19.
4. Wommack, "You've Already Got It," para. 9.

This goes against the grain of the entire biblical canon, where righteous people suffered not just as righteous people but *because* they were righteous. No one exemplified this principle more than Jesus, the only truly righteous person, who endured unimaginable suffering to fulfill the will of God. Jesus is the sufferer par excellence, but he is not supposed to be alone. Jesus told his disciples, "If anyone wants to follow after me, let him deny himself, take up his cross, and follow me. For whoever wants to save his life will lose it, but whoever loses his life because of me will find it. For what will it benefit someone if he gains the whole world yet loses his life? Or what will anyone give in exchange for his life?" (Matt 16:24–26). That doesn't sound like the prosperity gospel to me!

Suffering is not merely tolerated, but it is embraced by followers of Christ as an instrument of transformation that molds us in the image of Jesus. Paul, a great sufferer himself, once exclaimed, "My goal is to know him and the power of his resurrection and the fellowship of his sufferings, being conformed to his death" (Phil 3:10). Prosperity gospel practitioners are all about "the power of his resurrection," but they are decidedly weak on "the fellowship of his sufferings" and "being conformed to his death."

Alcorn put it this way, "We overrate health and underrate holiness. If physical health is our primary value, then why endanger it for a higher cause? While earlier Christians risked their lives to serve those dying from the bubonic plague, prosperity theology tends to encourage believers to flee threatening ministry opportunities so that they might cling to what they cannot preserve anyway."[5]

When we break away from viewing suffering through the lens of the prosperity gospel, we are set free to reimagine God's purposes in suffering. That doesn't mean we will always know or understand his purposes, but we can reject the theology that effectively places God in a box by suggesting that his only purpose for illness is to heal it. This leaves chronically ill sufferers trapped in that same box without the theological space to discover what God's purpose might be, not despite the illness and pain, but through

5. Alcorn, "Prosperity Theology," para. 22.

them. Whatever those purposes might be, they all coincide into one great purpose that never changes with the circumstances of life: knowing God for who he truly is.

WHEN GOD BREAKS HIS SILENCE

One of my three favorite books is *Till We Have Faces* by C. S. Lewis. It is one of those books that is ever-present in my consciousness. It's a brilliant retelling of the Cupid myth, and I hate to give spoilers if you haven't read it, but it has been out for seventy years! I will do my best to keep the spoilers to a minimum.

The story is told from the perspective of a princess named Orual, who will become queen if her father does not have a male heir. His last chance turns out to be another daughter, much younger than Orual, named Psyche. A lot happens from that point on, which causes Orual a great deal of loss and tragedy. She won't let anyone see her face for decades—she wears a veil—because her face is so ugly. Orual's misery leaves her looking for someone to blame, so she blames the gods.

Orual's understanding of the gods is what we now call Greek mythology. So, it doesn't seem like a Christian tale at all, but as Orual approaches the end of her life, she meets an elusive and mysterious figure. When she finally has the chance to speak to him, this is what she says: "I know now, Lord, why you utter no answer. You are yourself the answer. Before your face questions die away. What other answer would suffice?"[6]

It isn't very difficult to guess who Lewis is alluding to in this moment. It reminds me of a Bible story about a man who lost everything: his kids, his wealth, and his health; even his wife could no longer support him. He has three friends—there's a mysterious fourth friend who speaks near the end—but they prove to be miserable comforters. They push Job to the limits of his sanity by demanding that he confess the great sin that has caused God to punish him so severely.

6. Lewis, *Till We Have Faces*, 308.

However, Job will not play along. He knows he has done no such thing, and Job accuses God of a great deal of injustice. He wants God to show up and give an account for his suffering. He has all kinds of questions that he demands God answer. Then, all of a sudden, God does show up, but instead of Job questioning God, God questions him!

Job was not prepared for that. God asks Job a series of rhetorical questions, making the point resoundingly clear that there are many matters Job could not know and only God could. It is an impressive speech with the basic message of "I am God, and you are not." When God finishes questioning Job, he allows Job to respond, but like Orual in Lewis's story, the questions have all melted away. Instead, he says,

> I know that you can do anything
> and no plan of yours can be thwarted.
> You asked, "Who is this who conceals my counsel with
> ignorance?"
> Surely I spoke about things I did not understand,
> things too wondrous for me to know.
> You said, "Listen now, and I will speak.
> When I question you, you will inform me."
> I had heard reports about you,
> but now my eyes have seen you.
> Therefore, I reject my words and am sorry for them;
> I am dust and ashes. (Job 42:1–6)

KNOWING GOD IS OUR PURPOSE

God did not need to let Job know the reasons for his suffering. We sometimes think our situation would be more tolerable if we only understood the reasons we suffer. But despite what we may believe, these are not the answers we need. The whole point of Job's suffering was to defeat Satan's challenge that Job did not serve God for nothing (Job 1:9), but God never explained himself to Job. Instead, Job discovers that there are things only God can know, and that knowing God himself is the real answer he needed.

That same opportunity is available to you, though I hope you don't have to suffer to the degree that Job did to experience it. But the question is the same: will you serve God for no other reason than that he is God? If your response is, "It depends on what kind of God he is," then I recommend you take some time to meditate on what the cross of Jesus tells us about what kind of God he is.

I don't know a lot about the Westminster Shorter Catechism. I suppose there must be a longer one for there to be a shorter one! I may not know much about it, but there is one declaration from it that we should all know: "Man's chief end is to glorify God and enjoy him forever."[7] Suffering does not have to interrupt this chief end of humans. It can even play a role in helping us focus on the end that truly matters.

We all suffer to varying degrees. Following Jesus has never been a "get-out-of-suffering card," despite how prosperity gospel preachers frame it. Jesus framed it himself with the call to "pick up your cross and follow me" (Mark 8:34). Chronic illness is a difficult cross to bear, but we do not bear it without purpose. But that purpose is not directed toward some greater good you can measure. That purpose is powerfully articulated in the words of the apostle Paul: "My goal is to know him and the power of his resurrection and the fellowship of his sufferings, being conformed to his death, assuming that I will somehow reach the resurrection from among the dead" (Phil 3:10–11).

7. Westminster Standard, "Westminster Shorter Catechism."

REFLECTION QUESTIONS

1. How has your experience with chronic illness or pain deepened your relationship with God or helped you discover something new about yourself?
2. What is the "prosperity gospel," and how can it be especially harmful to people living with chronic illness or pain?
3. The author writes, "Suffering is not merely tolerated, but it is embraced by followers of Christ as an instrument of transformation that molds us in the image of Jesus." Do you agree or disagree with this statement? Why?
4. What kind of answer does Job ultimately receive from God in response to all his questions?
5. Do you find yourself needing more *from* God or *more* of God? How would you describe the difference?

Chapter Eight

The Gain of Living for Something Greater Than Money

WHEN MONEY STOPS BEING ENOUGH

As I write this chapter, my family is facing a financial crisis greater than any we have ever experienced. That's saying something. Our firstborn had an unexpected medical problem about the same time we realized our first home was a money pit. We managed to take some equity out of our second house to invest in what we thought was the safest investment possible, only to discover the investors were criminally irresponsible with our money (and thousands of others). We lost over $12,000, and the two principal investors went to prison. Not long after this, the housing market crashed, I got laid off, and the bank foreclosed on our house.

Our bad luck doesn't stop there, but you get the picture. Everything I mentioned above was *before* I had chronic illnesses. After thirteen years of living with unending medical bills, it has all finally caught up with us to the point that we can no longer meet all our obligations. I believe we can avoid bankruptcy, but many haven't been so fortunate.

In an article published in 2005, a team of researchers interviewed 1,771 people who had filed for bankruptcy in 2001, with a special focus on those who had done so due to medical bills. What they discovered was stunning:

> Among those whose illnesses led to bankruptcy, out-of-pocket costs averaged $11,854 since the start of illness; 75.7 percent had insurance at the onset of illness. Medical debtors were 42 percent more likely than other debtors to experience lapses in coverage.[1]

While these numbers are staggering, they are dated. Medical expenses have increased exponentially since then. To put it in perspective, consider this statement from an NPR article based on polling data: "A quarter of adults with health care debt owe more than $5,000. And about 1 in 5 with any amount of debt said they don't expect to ever pay it off."[2] I am going to go out on a limb and say that the "1 in 5" is often someone with chronic medical conditions. It is a bleak picture, but it is a personal one, too. We are being overwhelmed by crushing medical debt with little relief in sight. How can anything good come from such financial woes? Though we understandably seek financial relief that may or may not come, Jesus points us to a greater good: freedom from money's grip on the heart.

BREAKING THE SPELL

Jesus warns us that rust, moths, and thieves destroy earthly treasures. Therefore, he says, "Don't store up for yourselves treasures on earth" (Matt 6:19). Some of us may feel like the medical system qualifies as "thieves" that keep taking more and more, but Jesus is not giving an exhaustive list of treasure destroyers. He may have warned twenty-first century Americans about plunging markets, out-of-control inflation, and crippling debt.

Jesus wasn't only giving us practical advice. He was warning his first-century Jewish disciples about the allurement of wealth and the idolatrous compromises that come with it. Jesus' teaching on the perishability of wealth is relevant to all cultures and times. A few verses later, he says, "You cannot serve both God and money" (Matt 6:24).

1. Himmelstein et al., "Illness and Injury," 63.
2. Levey, "Sick and Struggling," para. 7.

Some of us may have been prosperous enough in our pre-illness lives that we were unwittingly living for money. We gave in to its power of seduction as a rival god vying for the throne of our hearts. It is hard to overstate just how dangerous the American culture is when it comes to the allurement of wealth warping our loyalty to Jesus. Likewise, the apostle Paul warns those chasing wealth in first-century Ephesus through his apprentice, Timothy:

> Instruct those who are rich in the present age not to be arrogant or to set their hope on the uncertainty of wealth, but on God, who richly provides us with all things to enjoy. Instruct them to do what is good, to be rich in good works, to be generous and willing to share, storing up treasure for themselves as a good foundation for the coming age, so that they may take hold of what is truly life. (1 Tim 6:17–19)

Many living for wealth are in real danger of not taking "hold of what is truly life." If we are humbled by our financial circumstances due to medical expenses and debt, then we can thank God that he has broken the spell of living for wealth, which robs us of life itself—in other words, life with him.

SERVING GOD OVER MONEY

If we have been freed from the power of money, then we are free to serve the living God. Many wealthy and resourceful churches and individual Christians have bought into the lie that we need money and health for God to use us, or even that they are hallmarks of God's approval. To the contrary, money and health can become stumbling blocks that get in the way of our dependence on God. How can we know God's strength when we are still impressed with our own?

A good friend of mine thinks some in his family may count his successes as less notable than theirs. He is thinking of their coveted and high-paying jobs. I don't know these other family members of his, but this man does more for our community and helps more children who are in trouble than anyone I know. He would not trade his success for theirs for all the money in the world. My friend has chosen what matters; if anyone thinks less of him for it, then they are still deceived by money. If money is a false metric for a successful life, what is the true standard?

When the author of Hebrews lists the four qualities of authentic conversion, wealth is not one of them: "For it is impossible to renew to repentance those who were once enlightened, who tasted the heavenly gift, who shared in the Holy Spirit, who tasted God's good word and the powers of the coming age" (Heb 6:4–5). I know this verse is central to arguments as to whether a genuine Christian can fall away or not, and if so, how can it be that some cannot be renewed to repentance? I also know that Christians are reading this book from differing perspectives on this question. I am not going to attempt to tackle those issues here. Instead, I want to focus on these four spiritual qualities as genuine characteristics of the truly converted and as indicators of the treasure in heaven that no one or no illness can touch.

The author of Hebrews uses four participles to modify the phrase translated in English as "It is impossible." In this case, the participles limit to whom that phrase is applied. The author is saying that if you have experienced these four things and then left the faith, then it is impossible to be brought back to repentance. Here's how *The Message* puts it:

> Once people have seen the light, gotten a taste of heaven and been part of the work of the Holy Spirit, once they've personally experienced the sheer goodness of God's Word and the powers breaking in on us—if then they turn their backs on it, washing their hands of the whole thing, well, they can't start over as if nothing happened. That's impossible.[3]

If we flip these four spiritual experiences into a positive statement of the full Christian life, the author illuminates just how thorough and profound the experience of knowing Jesus is. Each of these four descriptions of the Christian life is worth more than any financial security. Collectively, they form a sense of deep and

3. Peterson, *Message*, Heb 6:4–5.

abiding peace amid any worldly insecurity. Let's examine each one, respectively.

Who Were Once Enlightened

The word for enlightened is *photizō*. You can see the connection this word has to our English words, photo and photograph. The gold standard Greek lexicon, most often abbreviated BDAG, gives this definition in connection with our verse: "To make known in reference to the inner life or transcendent matters, and thus enlighten, give light to, shed light upon."[4] In our relationship with Jesus and as temples of the Holy Spirit, we are privileged to see reality differently than the rest of the world. We do not see God's creation in strictly material terms. What we experience in the body and what our limited resources are in the world are not the final words on our situation. Even if we face desperate financial strife, we have been enlightened to understand that it does not define us nor capture our future.

Who Tasted the Heavenly Gift

In the same amazing psalm that assures us "The Lord is near the brokenhearted; he saves those crushed in spirit" (Ps 34:18), the psalmist invites us in verse 8 to "taste and see that the Lord is good. How happy is the person who takes refuge in him!" The same word for "taste" is used in the Greek version of the Old Testament (the Septuagint) that is used in our passage from Hebrews. There is something tangible about experiencing the goodness of God. It is like you can taste it.

The author of Hebrews describes Christians as having "tasted the heavenly gift." The gift is not specified, but its origin is from heaven and not earth. It is natural to think of "the gift of the Holy Spirit" (Acts 2:28) or, relatedly, the gift of salvation as a whole (Eph 2:8).[5] Defining the heavenly gift may be challenging, but to taste it is to know it.

4. Danker and Bauer, *Greek-English Lexicon*, 1074.

5. Guthrie, *Epistle to the Hebrews*, 142.

Who Shared in the Holy Spirit

The author of Hebrews does not give a list as much as a multi-faceted prism for viewing the Christian life. Tasting the heavenly gift and sharing in the Holy Spirit cannot be separated from each other. You cannot taste the heavenly gift if you do not share in the Holy Spirit, and vice versa, but they emphasize different nuances of knowing God. Though the apostle Paul uses a different Greek word (*koinonia*), one cannot help but think of the last verse in 2 Corinthians: "The grace of the Lord Jesus Christ and the love of God, and the fellowship of the Holy Spirit be with you all (2 Cor 13:13). Again, intimacy with God, not just head knowledge, is emphasized. Encountering the Holy Spirit does not leave us unchanged.

Who Tasted God's Good Word and the Powers of the Coming Age

The final description of the transformed life again uses the word "tasted." And though there are four modifying participles in this passage, this last one receives two noun complements: "God's good word and the powers of the coming age." No one enjoys tasting something bad. What we have tasted from God's word is "good." Many people approach Scripture as something less than God's word or even as something distasteful, but the truly converted know and experience God's message as good.[6] Tasting "the powers of the coming age" is what empowers us to embrace our hope in Christ when all hope appears to have fled from this age. Those are dark times. That's why we need that taste of the age to come.

TREASURE IN HEAVEN

From the prophets to Jesus himself, and to his emissaries, God's word points to a coming eternal age where all things will be made new (Isa 43:19; Rev 21:5). The Christian's hope does not focus on escape through death but resurrection into immortal bodies that will make our present sufferings seem like a distant memory. Or

6. Guthrie, *Epistle to the Hebrews*, 143.

as Paul puts it, "For our momentary light affliction is producing for us an absolutely incomparable eternal weight of glory" (2 Cor 4:17).

These spiritual realities are transforming Christian experiences that intimately connect us to the divine and activate a hope that is far outpacing our worldly troubles. Paul is not diminishing the seriousness of those troubles but simply contrasting them to "the weight of glory." When things are going well, especially when life is aided by a surplus of money, we may forget the preciousness and weightiness of these heavenly realities. If financial trouble leads us to recover the ultimate value of knowing God, then we will start doing what Jesus said we should do:

> Don't store up for yourselves treasures on earth, where moth and rust destroy and where thieves break in and steal. But store up for yourselves treasures in heaven, where neither moth nor rust destroys, and where thieves don't break in and steal. For where your treasure is, there your heart will be also. (Matt 6:19–21)

Jesus does not say that our treasure will follow our heart; rather our heart will follow our treasure. It may be a subtle difference, but it paints a vivid picture of how what we invest in shapes our hearts. For many of us, financial struggle allows us to divest from the wrong priorities and start reinvesting in treasures of eternal worth. Then our hearts will begin looking more like Jesus'.

We all would like to think we would give up our wealth willingly if Jesus asked us to. Recall the story of the rich man in Mark 10:17–22. A man, who believed Jesus was the one who could answer one of life's most important questions, begged Jesus to let him know what he needed to do to have eternal life. When Jesus recited some of the important commandments, the rich man insisted he had kept all these from his youth. Yet, the man had the perception to realize that all that command-keeping wasn't enough. Otherwise, why bother the rabbi from Nazareth about it at all?

If you are familiar with this story, you know that Jesus finally gives him the hard word he needed to hear: "You lack one thing: Go, sell all you have and give to the poor, and you will have treasure in heaven. Then come, follow me" (Mark 10:21a). The man could not do it: "But he was dismayed by this demand, and he went away grieving, because he had many possessions" (10:22).

This incident prompted Jesus' memorable statement that it is easier for a camel to pass through the eye of a needle than for a rich man to enter into the kingdom of God (10:23). This stuns his disciples because they saw this rich man as one of the good guys. He appeared to them so evidently blessed by God. He was a good commandment-keeping man. If he can't be saved, then what hope is there for the rest of us? The rest of the conversation between Jesus and his apostles is worth reading, but something that gets missed is what Mark says about Jesus right before he makes this great demand on the rich man: "Looking at him, Jesus loved him" (10:21a).

Jesus was not trying to deprive or hurt this man. He loved him. Jesus was trying to free him from what was standing between him and God. We struggle with this story because we feel like either Jesus was being hard on the man or that we would fail this test as well. We don't consider that what Jesus does and demands is out of love.

I told you about my friend Billie in the previous chapter and how being robbed of his singing voice through a chronic condition led him to a place in his life where he knew he needed God. The financial loss in his situation played no small part in preparing him to meet Jesus. Sometimes, Jesus takes away what we wouldn't or couldn't willingly part with because he loves us. Peter demonstrates this perspective when he tells us that suffering and grief are like the refiner's fire for our faith:

> You are being guarded by God's power through faith for a salvation that is ready to be revealed in the last time. You rejoice in this, even though now for a short time, if necessary, you suffer grief in various trials so that the proven character of your faith—more valuable than gold which, though perishable, is refined by fire—may result in praise, glory, and honor at the revelation of Jesus Christ. (1 Pet 1:5–7)

Believing that our faith has greater worth than gold is easier to say than to live out in our materialistic society. Jesus' refining fire is for helping us, not punishing us. Jesus knows the things in our lives that need removing so that our faith "may result in praise, glory, and honor at the revelation of Jesus Christ." Do we trust him to do what is best to refine our faith? The loss of financial security is often one of the griefs we have to suffer so Jesus can bring out "the proven character of [our] faith" through his refining fire.

LIVING IN GOD'S PLAN A

In chapter 2, I shared the story of another friend of mine who was doing very well in her career and was financially rewarded before her company turned on her when she needed accommodations for her chronic health condition. RaeDeen was already a Christian when this happened, but she discovered her status and financial comfort had sown fear in her heart because she was afraid of losing it. Ironically, it was when she did lose it that she was finally free of her fear.

RaeDeen began to make progress working in real estate and as a grant writer. It was a slow start, but she took heed of Zechariah the prophet's warning not to despise the day of small beginnings (Zech 4:10). She decided at the outset of this new journey that she would not let her career be prioritized over her health. A third of her income still went to health care costs, but she resolved to trust God to provide even when she needed $17,000 for a stair chair.

RaeDeen learned to trust God in deeper ways than she ever had before: "I was always living in my plan B because I was afraid to live in God's plan A. I'm not afraid anymore." Learning to let go of our fear and to trust God even in the face of crippling losses is not easy, but it comes back to what we value above all. Where is our treasure? There we will find our hearts.

A few paragraphs above, we looked at what Peter had to say about the refiner's fire and our faith. In the two prior verses, he connects Jesus' teaching about treasure with the new birth when he writes of an imperishable inheritance:

> Blessed be the God and Father of our Lord Jesus Christ. Because of his great mercy he has given us new birth into a living hope through the resurrection of Jesus Christ from the dead and into an inheritance that is imperishable, undefiled, and unfading, kept in heaven for you. (1 Pet 1:3–4)

Jesus uses the word "treasure," and Peter uses the word "inheritance," but they are both speaking of that which is "kept in heaven for you," or our "treasure in heaven." No disease can ever touch our greatest treasure: our eternal inheritance as heirs with Jesus Christ.

Financial crisis and even ruin cannot take from you the things that matter most in life. These struggles can expose the lies surrounding money: that you are in control, that it makes you safe, and that it can be some kind of savior. Embrace the clarity that when all is stripped away, we see our true Savior with his hand mercifully reaching out to us to lift us out of our despair. Pray for help with your financial struggles. Seek out godly counsel and wise solutions as best as you can. Then leave it in God's hands and give thanks for the opportunity to invest in an eternal inheritance!

REFLECTION QUESTIONS

1. How have medical costs or debt affected the way you think about your financial future?
2. Why do you think losing prosperity or financial security can sometimes lead to a deeper dependence on God?
3. What does God let us taste in this life that whets our appetite for what is to come in the next life?
4. In this chapter, we read about RaeDeen, who said after losing her financial security, "I'm not afraid anymore." How do you think such peace is possible after losing so much?
5. What do you consider your true treasure—the one thing no disease, injury, or loss can ever take away?

Chapter Nine

The Gain of Kairos Time Over Chronos Time

THE AIR OF RESTFUL GRACE

In chapter 4, we acknowledged the massive loss of time we experience due to chronic pain and illness. Time is not a renewable resource for finite creatures like us. Once it's gone, it's gone.

However, that is not the whole story about time. Time is more than what is measured by units such as seconds, minutes, hours, days, months, and years. Not all moments are equal opportunities for purpose and significance. Life is meant for experiencing goodness and flourishing. How can we make the time we do have count for what really matters?

Who can forget Gandalf's famous encouragement to Frodo in *The Lord of the Rings* when Frodo lamented that he wished none of the horrible things that were happening had come his way: "And so do all who live to see such times. But that is not for them to decide. All we have to decide is what to do with the time that is given us."[1]

Gandalf's wisdom emphasizes the importance of accepting the realities we cannot control, such as the time chronic illness robs from us, and resolving not to miss the value of the time we do have. Chronic illness is a great tool for helping us recover a biblical

1. Tolkien, *Fellowship of the Ring*, 60.

view of time from a world that has warped it into a temple for the idol of productivity.

Most men and women are both told, implicitly and explicitly, that what is most important about them is what they can do or what they can produce. We all begin to take in this message as we strive to find our purpose in life, even with seemingly innocuous questions like, "What do you want to be when you grow up?" While our answers to this question change through the different stages of life and vary from a career-driven purpose to owning our own business or being an active parent, they are all tethered to an identity in doing or producing. "Time is money," we say, because we realize it is the only resource that we all have equally to devote to our chosen purposes.

Even if we don't all achieve our dreams, we still find value in the work we do, the money we make, and our involvement in an active lifestyle. Being busy is almost synonymous with importance or value. It feels wrong not to be doing.

Chronic pain and illness are wrecking balls to this illusion, which is rooted in the ideals of Western society. When I had my first hip surgery in 2012, I remember the acute feeling of not being able to do anything. For busy people, it may sound like a nice break, but after just one week of being laid up on the couch or my bed, I felt the encroaching cloud of depression. I craved being able to do something so that I would not feel useless.

Eventually, I recovered enough to be active and busy again. However, years later, I began to experience something worse (for me) than my chronic pain: chronic fatigue. I woke up exhausted and ended the day exhausted. In between, I had to lie down or even nap to get through my workday as a pastor. I had no energy for anything else. I distanced myself from my family, once more overwhelmed by the despair of a relentless daily routine that hardly felt worth the effort.

Even though I had studied Scripture for years, these new struggles became an impetus to realize that I had been reading the Bible through Western eyes. I had bought into the cultural lies that busyness and productivity are tied to value or even to God's approval, but the Bible tells a different story.

From the creation of the world to the ministry of Jesus and the words of the apostles, we see a picture of grace inviting us to rest. We see value that has nothing to do with productivity. When we let God define us instead of our world, we breathe the air of restful grace and discover that God delights in us simply as he made us, not because he needs us to do something for him. Here are three paradigm shifts that will enable us to breathe that air of restful grace.

1. SURRENDERING YOUR GUILTY CONSCIENCE

In Western society, and especially in American society, people are often valued by what they do and produce. This ableist mentality has left millions of chronically ill and disabled people on the sidelines. Our very sense of worth is under attack, sometimes by our own guilty conscience.

I gave a lecture on this topic for the Diamonds Conference, an online conference for the chronically ill, in June of 2023.[2] When I was talking with Leah, a Diamonds Conference volunteer, during a technology trial run the week before the conference, she asked me for prayer concerns. Before I knew it, I found myself asking for prayers that had to do with the very struggle that I was going to be talking about. I'm busy and stressed. I don't feel like I can get everything done that I want to or what I think other people expect from me. I don't even think I can get everything done that God expects from me.

When you throw chronic illness into the equation, the pressure only gets worse. Now there are doctors' appointments, prescriptions to refill, insurance matters to iron out, procedures and treatments to schedule, and you are doing all of this from a considerable energy deficit. Or to put it into chronic illness language,

2. For more information see diamondsconference.org.

you are trying to do even more with fewer spoons.[3] You try to keep up as long as you can, but chronic illness does not care how much you think you must do. You used those spoons to get through the workday? What now? Our kids don't always understand, "Sweetie, I'm tired," or "It hurts my shoulder too much to throw the ball." And the family's got to eat even when you have nothing else to give for the day.

Or maybe you're single and your friends are going out, and for the third time in a row, you tell them, "No, I can't tonight." You feel your friendships fading. Oh, you were supposed to volunteer at the local food bank? You barely have energy to eat your own food.

I haven't even mentioned the more drastic possible outcomes: giving up a career, becoming disabled, or requiring assistance to take care of yourself. So, when we take this American idol of productivity filtered through the Protestant work ethic—which influences more than just Protestants—we have a recipe for feeling awful about ourselves for all the things we can't do anymore. We start to feel like we are letting others down.

The Protestant work ethic is a complex theory developed by sociologist Max Weber in his book *The Protestant Ethic and the Spirit of Capitalism*.[4] I cannot delve deeply into this topic in this book. I am using the term as shorthand for the link between productivity and a particular Christian outlook. If we absorb that outlook, we begin to buy into a lie that we are letting God down. This leads us to doubt ourselves. *Am I really doing all I can? Is it really as bad as I am acting?* Truthfully, it is probably worse. You are probably doing more than you should because you are still trying to live up to expectations.

In a Lifeway poll about Americans and identity taken shortly before the pandemic, these were the top five markers Americans considered important to their identity: my role in the family (73 percent); the good I do (57 percent); what I have achieved (51

3. If you are unfamiliar with the "spoon theory," see Miserandino, "Spoon Theory."

4. Terjesen, "Weber Posits."

percent); my role as a friend (49 percent); and interests or hobbies (44 percent).[5] Every one of these named markers is affected by chronic illness and pain. If we do not know who we are before chronic illness strikes, our sense of worth will be ruthlessly attacked. Thankfully, God's word tells a different story and roots us in an identity that cannot be taken away by anything.

2. YOUR VALUE DOES NOT EQUAL YOUR PRODUCTIVITY

Each human is created with an irreducible sacred worth. Brokenness and weakness not only do not diminish this sacred worth but give God even more opportunity to show his grace and love toward us.

In the days of ancient Israel, there were competing stories about the value of humans, too. Some stories depicted certain humans as divine—the rulers or priests—while the rest of humanity was consigned to an identity of labor or even slavery. This is always the way of the empire. The extreme abuses of imperial rule reached new heights in Egypt. When Moses confronted Pharaoh on God's behalf to "let my people go" (Exod 7:16; 8:1; 9:1), he would not listen to the God of the Hebrews. He was "the Son of Ra" in Egyptian thought.[6] He had the divine right to enslave, and no other god could tell him otherwise—or so he believed.

Israel's creation story spoke of only one God, who creates not for exploitation but for blessing. Even the animals were blessed by God (Gen 1:22), but humans were created not as animals, nor are they divine. To be created rules out any possibility that we are divine, but we were not created as slaves, either. God declares our irreducible value when he links the creation of humans with his own image, and rather than making us slaves, he made us rulers:

> Then God said, "Let us make man in our image, according to our likeness. They will rule the fish of the sea, the

5. Earls, "Where Do Americans."

6. Nacumov, "Divine King."

> birds of the sky, the livestock, the whole earth, and the creatures that crawl on the earth."
>
> So God created man
> in his own image;
> he created him in the image of God;
> he created them male and female.
>
> God blessed them, and God said to them, "Be fruitful, multiply, fill the earth, and subdue it. Rule the fish of the sea, the birds of the sky, and every creature that crawls on the earth." (Gen 1:26–28)

From the very beginning, we are created with sacred worth, bearing the divine image of God, to rule this creation in his name and to be blessed by him. But the creation story doesn't end there. People were not the last thing he blessed:

> So the heavens and the earth and everything in them were completed. On the seventh day God had completed his work that he had done, and he rested on the seventh day from all his work that he had done. God blessed the seventh day and declared it holy, for on it he rested from all his work of creation. (Gen 2:1–3)

The Sabbath as a practice for Christians is a different discussion, but just as he had said three times that humans were made in his image, the narrator tells us three times what God did for the Sabbath: he made it holy. What does it say about God that rest is the final act of his creation? It supports the passage we quoted above from Gen 1:26–28. It confirms that God did not create us for only what we could produce. He does not need us as his slaves. He has created us in his image to rule with him over a creation blessed by his love and grace and to enjoy the rest (Sabbath) he so graciously invites us into.

Of course, we can make a good theology for work in Genesis as well, but disease, disability, and death had not yet intruded into God's design for us. When sin entered the world, so did all the abuses that lead to exploitation and the warping of God's good creation for our own ends. Consequently, value became tied to what we can do, and those who couldn't do were often ruthlessly discarded.

When we come to the words of Jesus and Paul in the New Testament dealing with work or how we use our time, we cannot forget that their words are deeply rooted in the soil of the same story. Redemption is "buying back" what was lost in the fall, including restoring a view of work and productivity that is not exploitative of the ones God created to bless.

3. KAIROS AND THE GRACE OF GOD

As Jesus is God in the flesh, it is no surprise that we see him offer rest as a blessing. He invites us, the weary and suffering, to himself:

> Come to me, all of you who are weary and burdened, and I will give you rest. Take up my yoke and learn from me, because I am lowly and humble in heart, and you will find rest for your souls. For my yoke is easy and my burden is light. (Matt 11:28–30)

This means reclaiming God's intended vision for who we are and why we are created. Jesus doesn't say there is no burden in following him, but that it is *light*. Jesus is not trying to exploit us. He does not unnecessarily burden us. But the messages we have received from our church leaders—people like me—have often sounded more like the ways of world empires instead of God's kingdom.

Even Paul can be misconstrued to say things that sound like busyness makes us more valuable. Consider the way we can sometimes interpret and apply Eph 5:16: "Making the most of the time, because the days are evil." *See, Paul says you'd better get busy, and there are a lot of you falling into sin because you aren't doing anything at church, and you are idle.* It isn't hard to see how a message of intended grace easily turns into a tool of manipulation. Most people who do this—and I have done it—probably unwittingly buy into the cultural narratives we have discussed already, but if we remove the filter of American productivity from Paul's message, we will see a message of grace embedded in Paul's words:

> Pay careful attention, then, to how you walk—not as unwise people but as wise—making the most of the time, because the days are evil. So don't be foolish, but understand what the Lord's will is. And don't get drunk with wine, which leads to reckless living, but be filled by the Spirit: speaking to one another in psalms, hymns, and spiritual songs, singing and making music with your heart to the Lord, giving thanks always for everything to God the Father in the name of our Lord Jesus Christ, submitting to one another in the fear of Christ. (Eph 5:15–21)

This is a loaded passage, but let's focus on verse 16. This section begins with "Be imitators of God, therefore, as dearly beloved children" (Eph 5:1). In the passage cited above, "making the most of your time" is not an independent phrase but modifies the command to "pay careful attention to how you walk." One of the ways we do this is by being intentional with our time so that we do not give evil a chance to triumph. The context is quite different from the idea that Paul means get busy and stay productive. It is more like Paul is saying, "Don't throw your life away." That's what getting drunk leads to (reckless living, verse 18).

We talk about time in diverse ways as well. It is the difference between telling my son, "I want the yard mowed by Friday," and telling him, "It's time for you to grow up." The first statement is *chronos* time, referring to chronological time like in "chronic" illness. The latter statement is *kairos* time. It refers to a decisive moment or opportune time. Paul uses kairos here, making the most of your kairos.[7]

Recall Charles Dickens's iconic opening to *A Tale of Two Cities*: "It was the best of times, it was the worst of times."[8] He doesn't mean 2:00 on a Tuesday. He's speaking of an age. You might miss an appointment (chronos time), but for the things that really matter in life, you do not want to miss kairos. In Eph 5:16, Paul is speaking about our lives as a whole. We are to be the kind of people

7. Danker and Bauer, *Greek-English Lexicon*, 497, 1092.

8. Dickens, *Tale of Two Cities*, 1.

who value our opportunities in this age of waiting on the return of Christ enough to be, as some translations have it, "redeeming the time" (e.g., Berean Standard Bible).

I experienced a profound confusion of these two different concepts for time when I was on a mission trip in Recife, Brazil. We had spent all week recruiting people to participate in our two-day intensive conversational English program, and when it was time to start on Friday, almost no one was there! I began to panic, but the American missionary who grew up in Brazil tried to put me at ease. He kept telling me that we would know when the time was right to start. I kept insisting that the time (chronos) to start was seven o'clock! Finally, I asked him, "How will we know when it is time to start?" I was told, "The Spirit will make it clear." Somehow people began arriving, and as the room filled up, I realized it was indeed time (kairos) to start! This intuitive sense of God's timing is exactly what Paul describes in Romans.

Paul writes in Rom 13:10–11 (NET), "Love does no wrong to a neighbor. Therefore love is the fulfillment of the law. And do this because we know the time, that it is already the hour for us to awake from sleep, for our salvation is now nearer than when we became believers." Some translations separate the call to love our neighbor from the admonition to "know the time" (kairos), but they are connected in the Greek. The NET quoted above does a good job of keeping these elements connected. *Knowing the time* or *redeeming the time* has nothing to do with how much work you can do. It has everything to do with loving God and loving others. The call to kairos is God's grace for us to prioritize what matters the most. Those of us afflicted by chronic (chronos*)* illness are sometimes best positioned to see what truly matters (kairos*)* to God, loving him and loving others.

LIVING BY GRACE INSTEAD OF THE CLOCK

Our value is rooted in our irreducible worth, and our identity is God's truth that we are created in the image of God and redeemed by the blood of the Lamb. Of course, I am not saying chronos time doesn't matter. When I was engaged, my fiancée gave me a picture of our wedding chapel. She wrote the date and time on it with a message saying, "Be there!" I can assure you that chronos time mattered in that message!

Some seasons are busier than others, often with very good things, and we are thankful for those seasons. But other seasons are unrelenting, frustrating our every attempt to be productive and to do the things we want to do. It is in these times that we most need to remember that God's grace is not tied to a clock or a bottom line. He has already redeemed us, and it is more important to him, and therefore to us, that we do not miss the opportunities to love him and love others rather than finishing a checklist of tasks. What energy we do have, let us invest it into relationships and blessing others. Yes, chronic pain and illness take away many social opportunities, but it also helps us focus on what really matters and making our time, our kairos, truly count.

REFLECTION QUESTIONS

1. How does being created in the image of God give you a deep and lasting sense of worth?
2. What dangers come with finding our value in productivity or achievement?
3. Why did God give his people the Sabbath, and what does that reveal about his relationship with us?
4. What is the difference between kairos time and chronos time? Which kind of time is usually in view when the Bible talks about good stewardship of time?
5. What is one relationship you could bless through an intentional investment of kairos time this week?

Chapter Ten

The Gain of True Friends

SPOTLIGHTING TRUTH

In chapter 5, we explored the devastating pain of losing relationships on our chronic illness journey. Some relationship losses are not the result of malicious betrayals but rather the effect of attrition caused by the loss of quality time with those we used to share activities with in healthier days. The losses of these relationships are painful, but many things can change the nature of a relationship, including chronic health issues. But there are those friends and family members who are never supposed to leave your side no matter what. When they abandon you because of the change in your health, it causes unspeakable pain, a pain that may even surpass the chronic pain you are living with.

However, your health challenges did not create the relational breakdown but rather exposed people who were only in it for themselves or, more generously, did not know how to be a good friend in that situation. The latter may be willing to learn. The former, sadly, have already moved on, leaving their hurting loved ones and friends behind. That does not have to be the end of their story—always leave the door open for repentance and forgiveness—but by assessing these relationships in their present status, you can think of your health situation not as a trigger for relationship breakdowns but as a spotlight that reveals what was real and what was never there at all. But that same spotlight will do something else as well: it reveals those who will never leave your side, no matter what.

THE VALUE OF A TRUE FRIEND

Proverbs 18:24 declares, "One with many friends may be harmed, but there is a friend who stays closer than a brother." Perhaps you knew what it was like to have many friends before your health struggles, and now you know the truth of this proverb. Harm can come to those with many friends, but have you discovered the other truth in this proverb? "There is a friend who stays closer than a brother" (or sister). The biblical witness appears to put a premium on the quality of a few trusted friends, who will never leave you, over having a great quantity of friends. Having many friends is a luxury, but a true friend is a necessity. The teacher of Ecclesiastes illustrates it like this:

> Two are better than one, because they have a good return for their work:
>
> If one falls down, his friend can help him up. But pity the man who falls and has no one to help him up! Also, if two lie down together, they will keep warm. But how can one keep warm alone? Though one may be overpowered, two can defend themselves. A cord of three strands is not quickly broken. (Eccl 4:9–12)

I know some who read this may feel utterly alone. You may believe you are the one to be pitied because you have "no one to help [you] up." If that describes you, I'm not saying this to shame you but only to name the ache and insist you were not meant to carry it alone. If you are lacking any true companions for your journey, you need a community, whether that is a church, small group, one trusted friend, or a support group like Broken and Mended, where you can be known and helped. We all need the support of people who have gone through similar experiences and upon whom we can lean and vice versa. Giving up is not an option. God himself said, "It is not good for man to be alone" (Gen 2:18).

If you are alone, know that isn't what God wants for you. Move into a space where you can discover friends who will help you up.

Virtual spaces are becoming common across all types of relationships. Nothing can substitute for sharing physical space and experiencing human touch, but that isn't always possible. Give yourself permission to embrace the tools you have at your disposal and know that, in God's hands, even less-than-ideal means may provide an ideal outcome.

For the friends you already have, it is important that you communicate your limitations honestly. It is easy for them to forget that you can't do the same things you used to be able to do that helped establish your friendship. It could have been as simple as sitting next to each other in church, and now you are watching church on a screen at home while your friend is off-screen somewhere in the audience. Let your friend know that you miss them and work together to find new ways to spend time together that account for your health limitations. Apps like Marco Polo, a video messaging app, can help fill in the gaps when you are not able to spend time together physically. I even started a support group on Marco Polo. I'm sure there are other similarly useful apps.

If you did not have close relationships with people before your illness, or those who were close to you no longer express the concern that is characteristic of a friend, you may need to take the initiative to find online communities in search of new friends. Being in a Christian chronic illness social media group is a start, but find a way you can interact directly with other believers who are going through what you are experiencing. We offer that opportunity in Broken and Mended through several different Zoom-based support groups. Consistent attendance and participation can lead to creating new relationships. Some feel like their appearance is not acceptable for video (i.e., they were not able to physically get themselves ready in a way they would normally desire for public situations). You can turn the camera off and participate as best you can. Anything is better than complete isolation.

Most of us are not completely alone. Whether you take the step to find a support group or not, take a moment to take stock of who hasn't left you. Don't let those who have left you rob you of appreciating those who haven't. For me, that person was Chris.

I had been friends with Chris since 1998, when I was a campus ministry intern in Denton, Texas, and he was one of the student leaders. We shared in all kinds of ministry together, witnessing God's transforming work in the lives of many, including our own. We went to Japan and China together on mission trips. We supported each other through numerous personal difficulties.

I remember the first day I told Chris that my x-rays revealed arthritis while I was still in my thirties. Around that time, Chris suggested we start talking on the phone weekly—we were a seven-hour drive from each other. Chris, who was healthy, wanted to walk with me through my chronic illnesses and intentionally planned to do so.

He didn't always understand the nature of my health problems, which led to a few disagreements. We worked through those because the value of our friendship was never in doubt, no matter what. Chris listened to my dreams about the ministry that would become Broken and Mended. He designed our original logo based on the Japanese art form of *Kintsugi*. Every time I see our Kintsugi bowl, I am reminded of Chris.

Chris wasn't just taken from me in 2019. He was taken from his two children, his parents, his siblings, and many other friends and family. The friend I lost was the one I talked with the most outside of my wife. We shared in each other's dreams and supported each other through life's disappointments and tragedies. I have longed to speak to Chris about Broken and Mended many times since his passing, and well, I would love to talk to him about anything at all.

Losing him left a void in my life I never could have predicted. I wonder if he's aware of what is happening in my life. I think about him having reached the finish line of this life and falling into the arms of his Savior. On days when the pain is bad or life is just hard, I am jealous of his current status. Don't get me wrong: I have much to live for and, God willing, many years to do it. The memory of Chris inspires me to press on when I don't feel like I can.

I read through *The Lord of the Rings* every decade. This past time was the first after Chris died. The relationship between Frodo and Sam is one of the all-time great literary friendships. When I came to the part of Frodo's departure from Sam at the Grey Havens, I was undone by what Frodo told Sam: "Do not be too sad, Sam. You cannot be always torn in two. You will have to be one and whole, for many years. You have so much to enjoy and to be, and to do."[1] So, I try to live the way Frodo exhorted Sam until those many years, however many they may be, are finally spent.

Losing a friend to abandonment or betrayal is very different from how I lost my friend. But my point is that when chronic illnesses wreaked havoc in my life, it only served to spotlight the true friend I already had. We need friends like Chris in our lives, those who will never leave us in our darkest valleys. The "friends" that left have been revealed to be exactly who they were all along. Let's appreciate even more those who would never leave and those whose friendship is shown to be the genuine article.

DISCOVERING OUR TRUE FRIENDS

Even before Chris died, I was forming a great friendship with Jim in my adopted hometown of Woodward, Oklahoma. We bonded over movies, books, and sports but eventually recognized we shared a kindred spirit in areas like theology and politics. From the beginning, Jim recognized the potential in what would eventually become Broken and Mended. His mother, Wilnetta, had struggled with debilitating and life-threatening chronic conditions for as long as he could remember. He saw firsthand the devastating toll chronic illnesses take on the whole family.

When I started Broken and Mended in 2018, Wilnetta was a charter member. Her health was never good enough to attend the sessions in person, but we were using Zoom in the pre-pandemic days. Wilnetta Zoomed in from hospital beds on many occasions, and when she talked, everyone listened and was encouraged.

1. Tolkien, *Return of the King*, 309.

Wilnetta passed away that following July, the same month that Chris passed away. I officiated Chris's funeral eight days after I had officiated Wilnetta's. Though Jim and I were already close, sharing in one another's grief bonded us even more. He had lost his brother in a tragic car accident in 2001. He is quite intimate with suffering.

After Chris died, Jim and I began to share in life's conversations even more. For many years, I had talked to Chris weekly on the phone. Now I was drinking coffee with Jim every Friday morning. Of course, a new friend or growing friendship can never replace the one lost, but standing beside each other through suffering and grief revealed the true nature of our friendship; it is unbreakable.

You have likely seen many friends come and go through the years. None of us can stay as close as we want with everyone. As we have acknowledged, you may have experienced friends or family members leaving you when things got tough. This kind of betrayal is hard to move past. It helps to remember that all of Jesus' friends left him when he was in his greatest trial. Judas betrayed Jesus. Peter, one of Jesus' closest friends, denied even knowing him. Jesus knows what it is like to be betrayed, denounced, and abandoned. Judas was a lost cause, but Jesus' resurrection changed everything. Once-faithless friends were restored to a relationship with Jesus. And, of course, Jesus would go on to call millions his friends in a family redefined through doing the will of his Father (Matt 12:48–50).

We aren't Jesus, but many of you may know the pain of deep betrayal. However, this subtraction of "friends" may lead to an addition (or revelation) of true friends. My wife, Katie, has never flinched at the prospect of dealing with my life-altering health diagnoses. Neither did Chris, nor has Jim, nor have other dear friends who bless my life abundantly. I know I am more fortunate than many when it comes to faithful friends and family, but I pray God opens your eyes and your heart to see those standing by your side, come what may. I hope you will seek out others who know what it is like to have an uncertain future and daily pain through meaningful Christian community.

BEING A TRUE FRIEND

A scribe tried to justify himself before Jesus by demanding that Jesus define "who is my neighbor?" You may know the parable Jesus told in response. Jesus would not let the scribe off the hook by narrowly defining the neighbor he had to love. Instead, he told the famous good Samaritan parable to strike home the greater point: *don't worry about who your neighbor is; focus on being a neighbor to anyone in need* (Luke 10:25–37).

Adapting that same principle, my encouragement is not to worry so much about who is being a true friend to you. We can't control the actions and faithfulness of others, but we can control our own. If we focus on being a true friend to those who need one, I have a feeling we will have all the friends we need.

Jesus' apostles and friends did eventually prove themselves faithful, but Jesus was the good friend who laid down his life for his friends before they ever grasped what it meant to be his friend (John 15:13). Jesus ended up with innumerable friends for all of eternity! But first, he demonstrated himself to be the true friend. The same gospel that reconciled us to God can also reconcile us one day to our friends who abandoned us. Whether that happens or not, in this life or the next, we can step into the lives of others—not despite our suffering but because of it—and be a true friend to them.

REFLECTION QUESTIONS

1. What has your journey with chronic illness revealed about the people in your life?
2. What new friendships—or deeper ones—have formed as you've continued to live with your health challenges?
3. Why is it more helpful to focus on being a true friend rather than on who is being a true friend to you?
4. How does Jesus show us the best example of friendship, even when his own friends failed him?
5. Who is someone in your life that might need an intentional act of friendship from you this week?

Chapter Eleven

The Gain of Glory

WHEN SHAME LOSES ITS AUTHORITY

In chapter 6, we discussed experiencing the loss of dignity caused by chronic illness and its connection to shame. I heard someone say recently, "Your dignity is gone as soon as you slip on that hospital gown." Some indignities are momentary inconveniences (putting on a hospital gown), and others can crush you with shame.

In my work with Broken and Mended, I hear about people's darkest periods in their struggle with chronic illness. Many of these people do suffer from intractable pain, but it is more common for me to hear about their experience of shame as the most anguished part of their stories. It was shame that forced them to recognize how much their health had factored into their identity. The father, who can't throw a ball with his pleading children or maybe even hold them in his arms, didn't realize how much he took those fatherly roles for granted until he experienced the shame of not being able to fulfill them. The mother, who has to retreat to her bedroom every night while her husband cooks dinner because she doesn't have the strength to sit up, let alone to help cook, is experiencing much more than physical pain. She's grappling with a loss of worth found in the different roles she desires to fulfill.

These humbling limitations are not good in themselves, but they do provide a better lens by which to view our worth. As I have covered throughout the book, our identity is rooted in being created in God's image and being redeemed by God's Son. We learn a greater dependence on God when we do not have all those other secondary identities propping up our sense of worth: father, mother, career, income, church work, etc.

However, I do admit that we need not only a better perspective on who we are in the present but a strong conviction that a great reversal of our health, and even death itself, awaits us in the future. This is the only way to defang shame in our lives. Shame does not get the last word. When shame is endured in faithfulness to Jesus, glory gets the final say!

THE PATH OF JESUS

In Heb 11, the author asks us to consider men and women who put their faith into action, often at great personal cost. The point was not that things eventually got better, but rather that these people did not get to enjoy the fruit of their faith while living on earth. Not only that, but even now, they are still waiting for the full realization of their faith. They are waiting on us! The writer of Hebrews tells us, "All these were approved through their faith, but they did not receive what was promised, since God had provided something better for us, so that they would not be made perfect without us" (Heb 11:39–40).

We often talk about those who have gone on before us as being made whole in God's presence, but what the Bible teaches is more nuanced. They cannot be made complete or "perfect" until we are reunited in the resurrection, but even in the interim, God honors these people the world tried to shame:

> Others experienced mockings and scourgings, as well as bonds and imprisonment. They were stoned, they were sawed in two, they died by the sword, they wandered about in sheepskins, in goatskins, destitute, afflicted, and mistreated. The world was not worthy of them. They wandered in deserts and on mountains, hiding in caves and holes in the ground. (Heb 11:36–38)

"The world was not worthy of them." The world treated these people with contempt, but they are vindicated by God. Even though these people lived before the time of Christ, Jesus is the linchpin that holds their future and ours together, as the book of Hebrews continues to reveal:

> Therefore, since we also have such a large cloud of witnesses surrounding us, let us lay aside every hindrance and the sin that so easily ensnares us. Let us run with endurance the race that lies before us, keeping our eyes on Jesus, the pioneer and perfecter of our faith. For the joy that lay before him, he endured the cross, despising the shame, and sat down at the right hand of the throne of God. (Heb 12:1–2)

Jesus is our trailblazer. He endured shame, even the shame of the cross, to ultimately sit at the right hand of the throne of God. To sit at God's right hand means that he is sharing in the glory of God. That same glory belonged to the Son before the incarnation. As the apostle Paul tells us in Phil 2:5, "Adopt the same attitude as that of Christ Jesus, who, existing in the form of God, did not consider equality with God as something to be exploited."

Regardless of how your Bible translates this difficult phrase—whether as something to be "exploited," "grasped," or "used to his own advantage"—the core truth remains the same: they all acknowledge that Christ surrendered some aspect of his divine status or privilege, to which he was entitled by his nature. He did this for the express purpose of becoming a "slave" (verse 7), and "he humbled himself by becoming obedient to the point of death—even to death on a cross" (8).

True, the story did not end there, but we cannot forget that the story of the glory of Christ runs directly through a shame-filled cross. We do not always instinctively associate the cross with its shame because we know why Jesus went there. But to hang on a Roman cross naked as a spectacle not only to watching crowds but to jeering demons as well was to embrace the shame of the cross. That is why Hebrews says Jesus "endured the cross, despising the shame" (12:2). To despise the shame does not mean he evaded it but rather embraced it as the path back to the glory of his Father.

Going back to Philippians, we see the same theme. After surrendering his right to equality with God, Christ humbled himself to the lowest station possible: a cruel death on a cross. But at the moment of apparent defeat, Jesus' Father intervened to change the ending:

> For this reason God highly exalted him
> and gave him the name
> that is above every name,
> so that at the name of Jesus
> every knee will bow—
> in heaven and on earth
> and under the earth—
> and every tongue will confess
> that Jesus Christ is Lord,
> to the glory of God the Father. (Phil 2:9–11)

GETTING BEHIND JESUS

As praiseworthy as the deeds of Jesus are on their own merit, neither Paul nor the author of Hebrews wrote these things just for the sake of information. Paul began his famous Christ hymn (Phil 2:5–11) by calling on Christians to "adopt the same attitude as Christ Jesus" (verse 5). The author of Hebrews directed Christians to run the race "keeping [their] eyes on Jesus" (Heb 12:2). Jesus' path of willing suffering and humiliation was not an isolated event in history. Yes, what Jesus accomplished is unique, but he expects his disciples to follow his example.

But if that sounds like bad news, you've missed the plot. Jesus' story did not end with suffering and shame. It ends with eternal glory. When we follow Jesus, we find a path that gives meaning to our suffering and shame, even if it doesn't explain it. Apart from Jesus, death gets the final word—for all of us.

So, our options boil down to two: follow Jesus down the road that necessarily travels through suffering to glory, or walk aimlessly down our own path with not even a glimpse of glory. If it seems like an easy choice, it's supposed to be! When we choose option one, shame loses its grip on us. To suffer while following Jesus releases our shame back to the one who bore it himself at the cross.

There are people in biblical times, just like there are many today, who suffer because of their Christian faith due to persecution. I acknowledge that the kind of suffering I am talking about is different and common to all people, to varying degrees, but it is still an opportunity for God to shape us into more Christlike people. What I am aiming for is not so much the reason for our suffering but how we suffer when we do.

Jesus is in no way punishing his disciples when he invites them down the same road he traveled, when he invites us to take up our cross and follow him (Matt 16:24–26). Dietrich Bonhoeffer wrote, "When Christ calls a man, he bids him come and die."[1] How can this memorable summary of Jesus' call sound like life when it centers around death? But an invitation to death is not threatening when it is the path to eternal glory. The apostle Paul understood this well. He tried to help the Corinthians to see it. Sometimes we need to see the invisible:

> Even though our outer person is being destroyed, our inner person is being renewed day by day. For our momentary light affliction is producing for us an absolutely incomparable eternal weight of glory. So we do not focus on what is seen, but on what is unseen. For what is seen is temporary, but what is unseen is eternal. (2 Cor 4:16b–18)

THE ETERNAL WEIGHT OF GLORY

Paul is not making light of anyone's suffering by naming it "our momentary light affliction." He is reflecting on his severe suffering, a point he has underscored to these Corinthians, who claimed his suffering was a sign of weakness, which, as it turns out, he was more than happy to embrace and even boast about (2 Cor 12:10). To boast in weaknesses is to turn shame on its head. It means we

1. Bonhoeffer, *Cost of Discipleship*, 79.

believe Christ took the greatest shame the world could throw at him and turned it into eternal glory.

We all experience embarrassment, but Christ bore our shame that threatened to strip us of our worth. We still suffer indignities and embarrassments, but they do not define us because we are moving in the same direction as Jesus: the path to eternal glory. This is why Paul can call our afflictions "light and momentary." Paul's own sufferings were extensive, but compared to "the eternal weight of glory," they pale in comparison, as will our sufferings and experiences of shame if we embrace them as the path to glory. Moments of shame are hard to completely eliminate as we wait for that final glory, but the point is not that you have to wait until then to experience considerable relief from shame. It is the knowledge that Jesus bore our shame on the cross that becomes our totem to remind us of what is true.

In Christopher Nolan's fantastic movie *Inception*, the characters intentionally invaded the dreams of others to plant ideas that the dreamer would believe originated in their own minds.[2] The risk was that you could lose the ability to distinguish whether or not you were still dreaming and get trapped in the dream. So, each character had a totem that allowed them to test whether they were awake or still dreaming. Cobb, the main character, had a spinning top for his totem. If he was still dreaming, it would keep spinning indefinitely. If he was back in the waking world, the laws of physics still applied. The top would begin to wobble before ending its spin and toppling over.

The word "totem" has a lot of uses, but I am using it here for something that reminds us of what is real in a world where truth is often distorted. The cross of Jesus is our totem, our anchoring truth, that reminds us of what is real, what is true. When feelings of shame overcome me, I need that totem to remind me that he has already borne our shame and that this totem points to the truth that we will reign with him in glory.

I told you about Rick in chapter 5. He is the former Toyota executive whose chronic back pain robbed him of his career. He

2. *Inception*, Nolan, 0:44:30.

endured waves of shame as his identity was stripped away from him. Rick was a Christian, but he was taking his worth from his career. I will not say, and neither would he, that God caused his extreme chronic pain to remind him of where his identity should be, but God certainly used that pain in Rick's life for that purpose.

However, God did not accomplish this through means of shame. Instead, Rick saw God's hand reaching out to him in compassion during his darkest and most hopeless period of his life. Even Rick's wife could not see any way forward in his current condition. She prayed, "Heal him or release him." Rick was praying a similar prayer—for God to make himself known in some way or to take him.

God answered Rick's prayer in a stunning way through two friends. First, without knowing Rick's prayer, his best friend told him, "During this time of elevated pain, God will make himself personally known to you." A few days later, Rick and his wife were hosting two couples for dinner. Rick felt so bad and hopeless that he did not want to be around anybody, but they went forward with their plans at the insistence of his wife, and thus set the stage for Rick's prayer to be answered.

One of the men, who didn't even know Rick that well, told him, "God had put you on my heart the night before. . . . God wants you to know that you are his son and that he sees you. You are a good father and a good husband." Rick took the words of these two men as messages of hope from God. He believed God had made himself known, and this allowed Rick to keep living. This message became Rick's totem that rooted him in the truth that chronic pain had tried to consume.

More came from that conversation that led Rick to seek treatment again, which resulted in an incredible amount of pain relief. Today, Rick only lives with a fraction of the pain he used to endure, but it is the message Rick received that resonates with me: "You are his son or his daughter." That is our identity as followers of Jesus. It is hard for shame to win the day over people who are convinced they are sons and daughters of God!

So, let me share one final Scripture from the apostle Paul. It applies to what I have been saying about suffering generally, but also about shame specifically: "The Spirit himself testifies together with our spirit that we are God's children, and if children, also heirs—heirs of God and coheirs with Christ—if indeed we suffer with him so that we may also be glorified with him" (Rom 8:16–17). Sharing the suffering and shame of Christ is the pathway to embracing our destiny as coheirs with Christ. When we realize this, we have nothing to be ashamed of because the one who bore our shame invites us to share his glory!

REFLECTION QUESTIONS

1. How can focusing on future glory help you deal with the shame you experience now?
2. Who are some people in your "cloud of witnesses" whom you imagine joyfully awaiting your arrival in eternal glory?
3. What path to glory did Jesus choose through obedience, as described in Phil 2:5–11?
4. Why must followers of Jesus also walk the path from suffering to glory that he walked?
5. What aspect of your current suffering are you most looking forward to seeing transformed into eternal glory when Christ returns?

Chapter Twelve

The Gain of Wholeness (Shalom)

WHEN HEALING IS NOT THE WHOLE STORY

While I was in Kenya in the summer of 2024, I heard testimonies from several people who said they were healed because of Broken and Mended. Honestly, I did not expect to hear "healing" testimonies from those using our materials and support groups. I am not sure if they meant physical or spiritual healing or a combination of both. If they meant physical healing, then praise God! Still, they are the exception, not the rule. Most of the people we encounter have come to terms with the reality that healing is not coming in the here and now.

This is controversial for some who come from "faith-healing" traditions. Many claim that God always wants to heal us, but we have dealt with this claim in chapter 8. Though I deny that it is *always* God's will to heal us from our diseases and ailments, I do not wish to suggest that I do not believe that God *can* heal. He does so in varying degrees according to his purposes, but any healing before the resurrection is temporary. The healed person will still decline in health and eventually die. This is a reality the faith healers tend to forget when they insist that God will always heal the one who has faith.

As I was writing this chapter, a friend with a dying father-in-law texted me to let me know his family member had been restored to the Lord. I don't know the details of that story, but I know it included praying together for God's forgiveness with his death imminent. He has refused any further treatment. He will die, but he will live again. And when he does, his healing will be complete. He will have *shalom.*

SHALOM

One of the first words that comes to my mind any time I think about the Hebrew language is the word shalom. It is a Hebrew word that translates into English roughly as "peace." But our English word "peace" is too limited because it often only conveys the cessation of conflict. It says nothing about the restoration of right relationships but only a pause in active hostility.

Shalom is much more. It includes the concept of restoration and harmony. It is a theological proclamation that all is well. The story of the Bible is about lost shalom and God's heroic efforts to restore it. When Adam and Eve sinned in the garden, shalom was disrupted between humans and God, man and woman, and between people and creation. All things were thrown into a state of slow decay and death. Nothing in all of creation escaped the consequences of "the fall."

In our current situation, we experience shalom in a limited capacity. The best of relationships struggle at times. Creation still rises up and kills its rightful rulers, and the majority of people live estranged from God. Because of this state, we should never take it for granted when we see shalom in action now. A person healed from his disease, a sinner returned to a right relationship with her God, a father and son reunited after a decade of pretending the other was dead—these are all signs of new creation, of shalom. Shalom is the way things are *supposed* to be. That we even know things are not the way they are supposed to be is evidence of a standard that is currently out of our reach, a sign of a loving God who wants to bless his creation.

In Cornelius Plantinga Jr.'s book *Not the Way It's Supposed to Be*, he calls the spoiling of creation through sin "the vandalism of shalom." Yet he adds, "Still, everyone of us does possess the *notion* in which things are as they ought to be" (italics in the original).[1] However, this is a pointless "notion" if God's story is just about what was lost. We know that is not the case. The great arc of the biblical story moves from creation to new creation, where things will be as they are supposed to be in an even fuller sense than it was in the beginning. Because this time, there will be no chance of us ever rupturing shalom again. Here's how John depicted that final shalom in Rev 21:1–4:

> Then I saw a new heaven and a new earth; for the first heaven and the first earth had passed away, and the sea was no more. I also saw the holy city, the new Jerusalem, coming down out of heaven from God, prepared like a bride adorned for her husband. Then I heard a loud voice from the throne: Look, God's dwelling is with humanity, and he will live with them. They will be his peoples, and God himself will be with them and will be their God. He will wipe away every tear from their eyes. Death will be no more; grief, crying, and pain will be no more, because the previous things have passed away.

This isn't just a great passage to be read at funerals (though it certainly is!), but it is a vision given to John so that the church will know that though this world is full of broken shalom, our destiny is wholeness with God, with each other, and with creation. We can scarcely imagine it. It is a faint and faded memory from our ancient past but also a vivid vision of our future.

We can endure a lot if we know that we are destined for a better future. Because this "notion" (to use Plantinga's word) is reflective of a deep reality from our past that points to our future, we look for the ultimate healing that far exceeds the most fantastical "faith-healing" story you will ever hear. Far from betraying a lack of faith in God's healing powers, it takes incredible faith to live through suffering with the hope of eternal shalom. This hope is not grounded in a philosophical idea but in the astounding claim that Jesus of Nazareth rose from the dead. Too many Christians fail to connect their own destiny with his in a shared resurrection.

1. Plantinga, *Not the Way*, 11.

THE RESURRECTION OF THE BODY

I was a full-time preacher for over twenty years before I began working for Broken and Mended. In my sermons and classes, I have never been anything but unambiguous that our bodies will be raised from the dead, just as Jesus' body was raised from the dead. I have been unambiguous because the New Testament is unambiguous. Even further, the belief in a literal resurrection of the dead is so integral to the Christian faith that Christians are to be pitied without it (1 Cor 15:19). However, people are often surprised when I directly insist the Christian hope culminates in the bodily resurrection. These encounters always leave me a little shaken. Why is it so difficult for this crucial Christian doctrine to establish itself firmly in our hearts and minds?

If you are new to Christianity, then this is good to know from the get-go. Jesus left the tomb in the same body that went into the tomb. I use the word "same" here to emphasize that there was no other body for Jesus to inhabit. Obviously, the body itself underwent a number of substantial changes. He was able to appear behind locked doors when he pleased, but the scars from his crucifixion were still visible (John 20:19, 27).

Paul makes this same point in 1 Cor 15. It is the same body that goes into the grave that comes out of the grave, but it is a transformed body that has shed its mortality for immortality (1 Cor 15:35–46). Paul describes Jesus' resurrection as the firstfruits of the entire resurrection (15:20). In other words, as Christ goes, so do we. If you deny the future resurrection, Paul says, we are saying that Christ has not been raised (15:13), which is tantamount to denying the gospel itself.

Paul also writes in Rom 8:23 that the children of God are awaiting "the redemption of our bodies." Christian hope is not an escape from our bodies or discarding a used-up shell once we are through with it; it is the unwavering conviction that not even our bodies are left out of God's great redemption.

Many Christians may struggle with believing this because we don't know how it works. How many dead are there with no longer any trace of their bodies? The rising popularity of cremation—and sometimes the financial necessity of it—makes some wonder if there's even a body still to raise. But we are not asked to understand it. We are called to trust in God's sovereignty and his promises. There is no doubt that a bodily resurrection is what God has promised. But this isn't like having to swallow your medicine! This is good news! As people who have bodies that hurt all the time, knowing God will redeem us where it hurts the most is an incredible reversal, turning bad news (hurting bodies) into good news (glorious, immortal bodies)!

Understandably, many are concerned about what happens when we die. As this book is not a treatise on all things pertaining to the Christian afterlife, I can only say that the New Testament consistently highlights the hope of rest and comfort while we await future resurrection (Luke 16:19–31; 23:43; 2 Cor 5:1–10; Phil 1:23; and others), but it is *explicit* that this is not our final state. Those dead in Christ are incomplete until the resurrection and the reunion with those still living (1 Thess 4:13–18; Heb 11:39–40). It is because of the resurrection hope that Paul can write, "Where, O death, is your victory? Where, O death, is your sting?" (1 Cor 15:54–55).

The Christian hope is not an escape from the body but a transformed body: perishable to imperishable, dishonor to glory, weakness to power, natural body to spiritual body, mortal to immortal. It is at our weakest point that God gives us the victory. From illness and pain-ridden bodies to glorified and immortal spiritual bodies, God will not let Satan win our spirits or our bodies.

I've shared about Wilnetta a few times in this book. Her story inspires me because of her steadfast grasp of God's promises about what is still to come. Wilnetta struggled with chronic illness and pain her entire adult life. It stole so much from her.

Toward the end, her body was but a frail representation of God's desire for her. When Wilnetta knew her time was coming, she wanted to talk about her new body. She looked forward to being at home with God before the resurrection, too, but what comforted her the most was knowing that *what was most compromised in this life will be most glorified in the next.* She understood the implications of the hope of Easter—resurrection hope. I pray you will have that same hope as well.[2]

THE NEW HEAVEN AND THE NEW EARTH

If what I said about the resurrection challenged your view of the Christian hope, this section will do so even more. But again, the purpose of this book is not a full-orbed presentation of Christian eschatology. I recommend Skye Jethani's small and informative book called *What If Jesus Was Serious About Heaven?* for further reading. For now, I will say that creation itself is not left out of God's redemptive plan (see especially Rom 8:17–25).

Whatever view of heaven (ultimate dwelling with God) you carry into this book, I suggest it will be far greater than anything you can imagine. We will not simply be raised from the dead to live again in this world as it currently is. In this world, there is no escape from pain, suffering, grief, and death. Our hearts long for something more.

We long for shalom, but its full realization is currently out of reach. Not every longing is to be indulged, but this intense longing for ultimate healing and for all to be well in our world comes from deep within the human psyche. From those depths, we recall the faint echoes of a paradise now lost, where God walked with man and woman in harmony and where everything was at peace (shalom) in God's creation.

The crucified and resurrected Messiah has inaugurated the new creation. He has begun with his people by making them a new creation in Christ (2 Cor 5:17). Once we become a new creation, the longing intensifies. We endure every hardship, not only recalling paradise lost, but with the growing hope that it has already been regained. No illness, pain, or even death itself can rob us of the destiny God has purposed for us: to reign with him under his shalom forever. Now we only have to wait for it. While we wait, we pray the ancient prayer, "*Maranatha*! Come, Lord Jesus!"

2. Portions of this section are adapted from Heflin, *Leader's Guide*, 15–17.

REFLECTION QUESTIONS

1. Recall a moment of shalom in your life. When have you witnessed a powerful glimpse of restoration?
2. What is a moment of shalom you long for that you know will have to wait until the last day, when Christ renews all things?
3. How does the deep sense within us of how things are supposed to be point toward the future when everything will finally be as it should?
4. How does Jesus' resurrection transform our deepest longings into a confident expectation that they will one day be fulfilled?
5. How can the hope of the resurrection and the promise of "a new heaven and a new earth" encourage you on days when shalom feels out of reach?

Epilogue

Paradise Regained

. . . now thou hast avenged
Supplanted Adam, and by vanquishing
Temptation, hast regained lost Paradise,
And frustrated the conquest fraudulent.
—*Paradise Regained*[1]

The theme for this book, Paradise Lost and Paradise Regained, came into my mind before I ever read John Milton's classic poems about what was lost in the garden of Eden and how Christ has gone about rectifying it. Of course, the theme was inspired by those well-known titles, but when I did read them, I was surprised to discover that *Paradise Regained* does not focus directly on the redemptive work of Christ or the consummation of his kingdom at the end of history. Instead, Milton focuses on the temptations in the wilderness that took place at the beginning of Jesus' ministry.

Milton was not suggesting that Christ's work was complete at the end of that event but that the temptations provided the perfect

1. Milton, *Paradise Lost*, 397.

contrast to the failure of Adam and Eve in the garden. They were in place of beauty and harmony. They had all they could ever need and should ever want. They had every advantage over their adversary. Satan is much more effective when he can prey on deprivation, but they still failed, with catastrophic consequences. These catastrophic consequences include the focus of this book: disease and chronic pain, harbingers of death.

By contrast, Jesus had none of those advantages. He was at the extreme point of deprivation after fasting in the wilderness for forty days. Instead of the comfort of a shady garden, he was exposed to the elements and the wild animals. After fasting for forty days, Jesus was physically at his weakest when Satan visited him with those three temptations. Milton's poem presents an imaginative vision of why these temptations were particularly enticing and how Jesus was able to claim victory, foreshadowing the success of his entire mission and ultimately the regaining of paradise. That mission reached its fulfillment not in a garden or a wilderness but on a cross.

When the criminal crucified next to Jesus (commonly referred to as the "thief on the cross") asked Jesus to remember him when he came into his kingdom, Jesus replied, "Today, you will be with me in Paradise" (Luke 23:43). The word translated "paradise" meant garden in normal contexts,[2] but this was anything but a normal context. When Jesus tells a dying man that he will be in paradise, Jesus could only mean the paradise of God, which had been lost in Adam and Eve's downfall. And it was here, at the cross, where Jesus regained what had been lost, which was confirmed in his subsequent resurrection and ascension.

Living with chronic illnesses and other painful health conditions is much more akin to Jesus in the wilderness than Adam in the garden. We, too, experience deprivation caused by chronic health conditions that rob us of what we hoped our lives would be. Satan sits ready to pounce through discouragement and despair, or, as the apostle Peter wrote, "Your adversary the devil is prowling around like a roaring lion, looking for anyone he can devour" (1

2. Morris, *Luke*, 359.

Pet 5:8). That's why we need Jesus, the lion of the tribe of Judah (Rev 5:5), to stand between us and the devouring lion.

Jesus is uniquely qualified to save and sustain us as the one who has suffered in solidarity with suffering humanity but also as the one who has overcome the world (John 16:33). There's no avoiding this wilderness, but if we have to go into the wilderness—a long way from paradise—then let us go with the one who has already been victorious there. For his victory will be ours. So, let's pray for the strength to get through one more day, and then we will do it again tomorrow.

Bibliography

Alcorn, Randy. "Prosperity Theology: How the Health and Wealth Gospel Perverts Our View of Evil and Suffering." Eternal Perspective Ministries, Mar 25, 2010. https://www.epm.org/resources/2010/Mar/25/prosperity-theology-excerpt-if-god-good/.

American Psychiatric Association. "Chronic Pain and Mental Health Often Interconnected." Psychiatry.org, Nov 13, 2020. https://www.psychiatry.org/news-room/apa-blogs/chronic-pain-and-mental-health-interconnected.

Bonhoeffer, Dietrich. *The Cost of Discipleship*. Translated by R. H. Fuller and Irmgard Booth. 2nd ed. New York: Macmillan, 1959.

Capra, Frank, dir. *It's a Wonderful Life*. Los Angeles: Liberty, 1946.

Centers for Disease Control and Prevention. "Fast Facts: Health and Economic Costs of Chronic Conditions." 2025. https://www.cdc.gov/chronic-disease/data-research/facts-stats/index.html.

Chapman, Gary. *The Five Love Languages: How to Express Heartfelt Commitment to Your Mate*. Chicago: Northfield, 1995.

Christian Study Bible. Nashville: Holman, 2017.

Cleveland Clinic. "Suicidal Ideation: What It Is, Causes, Treatment & Types." Last updated July 23, 2024. https://my.clevelandclinic.org/health/symptoms/suicidal-ideation.

Cuncic, Arlin. "What Is the Holmes and Rahe Stress Scale?" Verywell Mind, Nov 17, 2022. https://www.verywellmind.com/what-is-the-holmes-and-rahe-stress-scale-6455916.

Danker, Frederick W., and Walter Bauer. *A Greek-English Lexicon of the New Testament and Other Early Christian Literature*. 3rd ed. Chicago: University of Chicago Press, 2000.

Dickens, Charles. *A Christmas Carol*. London: Chapman & Hall, 1843.

———. *A Tale of Two Cities*. London: Chapman & Hall, 1859.

Duffer, Matt, and Ross Duffer, creators. *Stranger Things*. Season 4. Los Gatos, CA: Netflix, 2022.

Earls, Aaron. "Where Do Americans Find Their Identity?" Lifeway Research, July 30, 2019. https://research.lifeway.com/2019/07/30/where-do-americans-find-their-identity/.

Fleming, Victor, dir. *The Wizard of Oz.* Los Angeles: Metro-Goldwyn-Mayer, 1939.

Furman, Dave. *Being There: How to Love Those Who Are Hurting.* Leyland, England: EP, 2016.

Guthrie, Donald. *The Epistle to the Hebrews: An Introduction and Commentary.* Grand Rapids: Eerdmans, 2002.

Halpert, Julie. "Chronic Disease, Your Healthy Spouse, and Sex." HealthCentral, Mar 21, 2022. https://www.healthcentral.com/article/chronic-disease-your-healthy-spouse-and-sex.

Harrison, Jeremy. *Rethinking Depression.* Self-published, CreateSpace, 2016.

Hartley, John E. *Genesis: New International Biblical Commentary.* Peabody, MA: Hendrickson, 2000.

Heflin, David. "Chronic Illness and the Loss of Dreams: A Conversation with Bethany Honaker." *In The Seams*, podcast, season 2, episode 6, Dec 15, 2022. https://rss.com/podcasts/intheseams/1267341/.

———. "Interview with Remain Founders Aren and Trina Bahadourian." *In The Seams*, podcast, season 3, episode 6, Aug 30, 2024. https://rss.com/podcasts/intheseams/1635956/.

———. *Leader's Guide: Chronic Illness and Pain Support Group Resource.* Vol. 2. Woodward, OK: Broken and Mended Incorporated, 2024.

Himmelstein, David U., et al. "Illness and Injury as Contributors to Bankruptcy." *Health Affairs* 24 (2005) 63–73. https://doi.org/10.1377/hlthaff.w5.63.

Holman Christian Standard Bible. *Holy Bible: The Old & New Testaments.* UltraThin Large Print Reference ed. Nashville: Holman, 2004.

Jethani, Skye. *What If Jesus Was Serious About Heaven?* Chicago: Moody, 2023.

Keller, Timothy. *Walking with God Through Pain and Suffering.* New York: Penguin, 2016.

Levey, Noam. "Sick and Struggling to Pay: 100 Million People in the U.S. Live with Medical Debt." NPR, June 16, 2022. https://www.npr.org/sections/healthshots/2022/06/16/1104679219/medical-bills-debt-investigation.

Lewis, C. S. *Mere Christianity.* New York: Simon & Schuster, 1996.

———. *Till We Have Faces: A Myth Retold.* London: Geoffrey Bles, 1956.

Mental Health America. "Chronic Pain and Mental Health." 2024. https://mhanational.org/chronic-pain-and-mental-health.

Milton, John. *Paradise Lost and Paradise Regained.* New York: Start, 2012.

Miserandino, Christine. "The Spoon Theory." But You Don't Look Sick, 2003. https://web.archive.org/web/20191117210039/https://butyoudontlooksick.com/articles/written-by-christine/the-spoon-theory/.

Morris, Leon. *Luke: The Tyndale New Testament Commentaries.* Grand Rapids: Eerdmans, 2002.

Moses, H. "Chronos—The Primordial Greek God of Time and Cosmic Creation." History and Myths, Oct 23, 2025. https://www.historyandmyths.com/2025/10/chronos-greek-god-of-time.html.

Nacumov, Anabel. "The Divine King: The Myth of the Pharaoh as the Son of Ra." Egypt Mythology, Sept 17, 2024. https://egyptmythology.com/the-divine-king-the-myth-of-the-pharaoh-as-the-son-of-ra/.

Nolan, Christopher, dir. *Inception*. Warner Bros. Pictures, 2010.

Nusbaum, Margaret R. H., et al. "Chronic Illness and Sexual Functioning." *American Family Physician* 67:2 (2003) 347–54. https://www.aafp.org/pubs/afp/issues/2003/0115/p347.html.

Pemberton, Glenn. *Hurting with God: Learning to Lament with the Psalms*. Abilene, TX: Abilene Christian University Press, 2016.

Peterman, Gerald W., and Andrew J. Schmutzer. *Between Pain and Grace: A Biblical Theology of Suffering*. Chicago: Moody, 2012.

Peterson, Eugene H. *The Message*. Colorado Springs: NavPress, 2013.

Piper, John. "Can Christians Be Depressed?" Desiring God, Dec 19, 2007. https://www.desiringgod.org/interviews/can-christians-be-depressed.

Plantinga, Cornelius. *Not the Way It's Supposed to Be: A Breviary of Sin*. Grand Rapids: Eerdmans, 1999.

Solomon, Marty. "Letting Go." *The BEMA Podcast*, episode 9, Nov 17, 2016. https://podcasts.apple.com/us/podcast/9-letting-go/id1148115183?i=1000377965809.

Stetzer, Ed. "The Christian Struggle with Mental Illness." The Baptist Convention of Iowa. https://bciowa.org/the-christian-struggle-with-mental-illness/.

Terjesen, Nancy Conn. "Weber Posits the Protestant Ethic." Research Starters, 2023. https://www.ebsco.com/research-starters/religion-and-philosophy/weber-posits-protestant-ethic.

Themelis, Kristy, et al. "Mental Defeat and Suicidality in Chronic Pain: A Prospective Analysis." *The Journal of Pain* 24:11 (June 1, 2023) 2079–92. https://doi.org/10.1016/j.jpain.2023.06.017.

Tolkien, J. R. R. *The Lord of the Rings: The Fellowship of the Ring*. New York: Houghton Mifflin, 1987.

———. *The Return of the King: Being the Third Part of the Lord of the Rings*. New York: Houghton Mifflin, 1994.

Totenberg, Nina. "'She Really Didn't Give Up': Remembering the Life and Career of RBG." By Hari Sreenivasan. *News Weekend*, PBS. Sept 19, 2020.

Walton, Sarah. "Frozen in Grief: The Pain of Ambiguous Loss." Set Apart, May 11, 2021. https://setapart.net/2021/05/11/frozen-in-grief-the-pain-of-ambiguous-loss-4/.

Westminster Standard. "The Westminster Shorter Catechism." https://thewestminsterstandard.org/westminster-shorter-catechism/.

Wetherell, Kristen, and Sarah Walton. *Hope When It Hurts: Biblical Reflections to Help You Grasp God's Purpose in Your Suffering*. Grand Rapids: Zondervan, 2016.

Whitbourne, Susan Krauss. "When Praise Is a Problem." Psychology Today, Feb 23, 2019. https://www.psychologytoday.com/us/blog/fulfillment-at-any-age/201902/when-praise-is-a-problem.

Wommack, Andrew. "You've Already Got It." Andrew Wommack Ministries. https://www.awmi.net/browse-teaching/youve-already-got-it/?mode=video.

Zahnd, Brian. *The Wood Between the Worlds: A Poetic Theology of the Cross.* Downers Grove, IL: InterVarsity, 2024.

Scripture Index

OLD TESTAMENT

Genesis

Exodus

Deuteronomy

Job

Psalms

Proverbs

Ecclesiastes

Isaiah

Jeremiah

Zechariah

NEW TESTAMENT

Matthew

Mark

Luke

John

Acts

Romans

1 Corinthians

2 Corinthians

Ephesians

www.ingramcontent.com/pod-product-compliance
Lightning Source LLC
LaVergne TN
LVHW012332100826
845148LV00017B/2125

* 9 7 9 8 3 8 5 2 7 3 2 1 8 *